The Richmond Guide to
Praying the Liturgy of the Hours

*The Richmond Guide to*
# PRAYING THE
# LITURGY OF THE HOURS

RAYMOND LLOYD RICHMOND, PH.D.

ISBN-13: 978-1523738809
ISBN-10: 1523738804

# CONTENTS

# PREFACE

Because we do not experience a normal sensory perception of God, to live a properly ordered and directed holy life it is necessary to maintain a constant mental contact with God through prayer.

Our time in prayer, therefore, is the only time, in this life, when we can live in holiness. How sad that so many of Christ's own anointed treat Him so carelessly as to neglect simple, heartfelt prayer in which we speak intimately to God as we would speak to another trusted person.

If you constantly open your heart to God in spontaneous prayer, you will be immune to feelings of loneliness, of abandonment, of anxiety, of depression, and of all other problems with psychological causes. Yes, you will have to endure the heavy weight of living in the midst of the world's apostasy and sacrilege—but even that is anguish, not depression. On the other hand, if you neglect this prayerful communication with God you will be afflicted with all the untreated wounds of your own psychological emptiness.

For some persons—especially those wounded by

childhood abuse or neglect—the greatest obstacle to prayer is the irrational (that is, unconscious) belief that they are such despicable persons that God has totally abandoned them and refuses to hear any pleas for help. Although this belief is refuted by the Bible itself (e.g., 1 Timothy 2:4), such a belief derives psychologically from a confusion of God with the "Other" (i.e., the social world around us). In truth, the social world, at its best, is completely indifferent to our welfare, and, at its worst, it "sees" us only as objects to be manipulated for its own satisfaction. In other words, it is not God's rejection of you but *sin itself*—the rejection of God by the "Other"—that has abused you.

Therefore, the first step to prayer must be a *turning back* to your baptismal promises to renounce the world and Satan and to trust completely in God's protection; all genuine prayer, at its core, requires a sincere willingness to die to the world—the "Other" that seeks your spiritual destruction—in order to be resurrected into everlasting life.

Prayer should be a constant reminder of the presence of God and a continuing act of purification, not dry intellectual superstition and pride. Trying to pray without first detaching yourself from the false attractions of the world is like trying to drive a car with four flat tires.

Accordingly, as the *Catechism of the Catholic Church* explains (§ 2626-2643), prayer has several different aspects: *praise* (recognition of God not so much because of what He does *for* us but simply because He *is*), *thanksgiving* (simple gratitude for Christ's work of redemption and its personal effects on us), *adoration* (acknowledging our helplessness and humility in the presence of God's glory), *intercession* (pleading for the welfare of others), and *petition* (pleading for our needs as an expression of our hope and desire in all things that "Thy Kingdom come").

The surest approach to learning to pray properly is to instill in your heart a deep sorrow for sin (both yours and that of others) while desiring to be freed from the illusions of your own identity. Then confirm this desire by fasting; that is, by making sacrifices of time, food, and other personal pleasures. And then sustain this desire by constantly speaking to God as you would to a trusted master, telling Him everything you are experiencing and asking Him for help and guidance in accomplishing every task before you.

### Praying Constantly

We should all, then, learn to pray constantly—as our Lord Jesus Christ advised us (Luke 18:1)—in both *vocal prayer*, which is the recitation of the Church's "standard" prayers, and *mental prayer*, which has three dynamically intertwined components: a quiet, internal *meditation* (i.e., a deliberate thinking about divine things); *contemplation* (i.e., a surrendering to the experience of divine love); and spontaneous *communication* with God (i.e., constantly being aware of God's presence, and asking for His help, in all that you experience in every moment.

Therefore, in praying constantly, we bring our minds into our hearts, such that our thoughts are constantly attuned to the presence of God, and our hearts are constantly inflamed with love for God and concern for the salvation of our neighbors.

### Vocal Prayer and Mental Prayer

Saint Teresa of Avila spoke constantly about the difference between vocal prayer and mental prayer. She also spoke very carefully about this difference. Because of the many abuses resulting from the illuminists—or *alumbrados*—of Teresa's time, many theologians looked on mental prayer with suspicion, fearing that it would result in a contempt for vocal prayer, along with a contempt for the liturgy, ceremonies, and rituals of the Church.

But, psychologically speaking, Saint Teresa got it right.

All prayer, she said, begins with vocal prayer—such as the *Our Father* and the *Hail Mary*—and then, by meditating on the meaning of what is being said, even *as* it is being said, the soul will effectively be led to mental prayer. And not just that, but in the quiet moments between periods of vocal prayer—even while performing our daily work—the soul should be filled with contemplative mental prayer of pure, timeless love.

So, in regard to vocal prayer and mental prayer, it's not a matter of either-or. When the soul struggles through darkness, it needs the beauty of mental prayer to cheer its heart and help it along. But it also needs the discipline of vocal prayer to keep it on the true path, lest it decide to chase off after alluring lights in the distance and be lost forever.

> Therefore, you need a strong warning. Through my experience with Catholic psychology, I can guarantee that you will often perceive things in prayer that are nothing but your own unconscious wish-fulfillment fantasies. Therefore, you have only one protection against spiritual destruction:

> *Reject anything that contradicts Scripture or Tradition or the Magisterium (teaching) of the Church.*

# 1    LITURGICAL SEASONS

---

## *Advent*

The liturgical year begins with Evening Prayer I of the First Sunday of Advent. The season of Advent continues through the four Sundays of Advent and ends at Christmas Eve.

Advent is a time of preparation, through fasting and prayer, for Christmas. Even though Christ was actually born over 2000 years ago, during Advent we prepare our hearts to "receive" Jesus into the world each year as a light to the nations, at a time when our calendar is reaching its darkest period. Advent is also a time of looking forward to Christ's Second Coming in the last days.

## *Christmas*

At Christmas we celebrate the Word become flesh, coming to dwell among us as the light of the human race, just after the darkest point of the solar year. Christmas, therefore, is a holy day second only to Easter.

The *Octave of Christmas* (*octave* means eight; hence the octave of Christmas lasts for eight days) begins with Christmas day and ends after the Solemnity of Mary, Mother of God, on January 1.

Traditionally, the *Twelve Days of Christmas* begins on Christmas and ends on Epiphany (in times past called Little Christmas), whose traditional date is January 6. Now that the new calendar (in some countries such as the US) transfers Epiphany to the Sunday between January 2 and January 8, the time between Christmas and the celebrated date of Epiphany varies, so the significance of those traditional twelve days has been lost.

Usually, the season of Christmas ends, and Ordinary Time begins, after Evening Prayer II of the Baptism of the Lord, which, according to the new calendar, now occurs on the next Sunday after January 6. But if the Sunday celebration of Epiphany occurs on January 7 or January 8, then the Baptism of the Lord is transferred to the Monday after, and Ordinary time begins that Monday.

### About the Christmas Season

The daily office for the days within the Octave of Christmas is complicated because each of these days has specific instructions for the Office of Readings,

Morning Prayer, and Daytime Prayer. On December 26 the feast of St. Stephen is celebrated; on December 27 the feast of St. John, Apostle and Evangelist is celebrated; and on December 28 the feast of the Holy Innocents is celebrated; then, December 29, 30, and 31 are, respectively, the Fifth Day, Sixth Day, and Seventh Day in the Octave of Christmas—and each of these days has unique instructions for its celebration. Evening Prayer for each of these days, however, comes from Evening Prayer II of Christmas.

As an additional complication, when Christmas occurs on a Sunday, the Feast of the Holy Family, which is usually celebrated on the Sunday in the Octave of Christmas, is celebrated on December 30, thus preempting the Sixth Day in the Octave of Christmas.

Furthermore, although Mary, Mother of God is always celebrated on January 1, celebrations for the days between January 2 and Epiphany all vary depending on the day of the week on which Christmas occurs. Moreover, when Epiphany is not celebrated on January 6 but is transferred to the Sunday between January 2 and January 8, the date of that Sunday itself depends on the day of the week on which Christmas occurs.

Here, then, is a summary of how things fall out (when Epiphany is transfered to a Sunday) according to the day of the week on which Christmas occurs.

- When Christmas occurs on a *Sunday*, the Holy Family is celebrated on Friday, December 30. There is a Monday through Saturday before Epiphany, Epiphany is celebrated on Sunday, January 8, and there are no weekdays after Epiphany. The Baptism of the Lord is celebrated on Monday, January 9.

- When Christmas occurs on a *Monday*, the Holy Family is celebrated on Sunday, December 31. There is a Tuesday through Saturday before Epiphany, Epiphany is celebrated on Sunday, January 7, and there are no weekdays after Epiphany. The Baptism of the Lord is celebrated on Monday, January 8.

- When Christmas occurs on a *Tuesday*, the Holy Family is celebrated on Sunday, December 30. There is a Wednesday, Thursday, Friday, and Saturday before Epiphany, Epiphany is celebrated on Sunday, January 6, and there is a Monday through Saturday after Epiphany. The Baptism of the Lord is celebrated on Sunday, January 13.

- When Christmas occurs on a *Wednesday*, the Holy Family is celebrated on Sunday, December 29. There is a Thursday, Friday, and Saturday before Epiphany, Epiphany is celebrated on Sunday, January 5, and there is a Monday through Saturday after Epiphany. The Baptism of the Lord is celebrated on Sunday, January 12.

- When Christmas occurs on a **Thursday**, the Holy Family is celebrated on the following Sunday, December 28. There is a Friday and Saturday before Epiphany, Epiphany is celebrated on Sunday, January 4, and there is a Monday through Saturday after Epiphany. The Baptism of the Lord is celebrated on Sunday, January 11.

- When Christmas occurs on a **Friday**, the Holy Family is celebrated on the following Sunday, December 27. There is a Saturday before Epiphany, Epiphany is celebrated on Sunday, January 3, and there is a Monday through Saturday after Epiphany. The Baptism of the Lord is celebrated on Sunday, January 10.

- When Christmas occurs on a **Saturday**, the Holy Family is celebrated the next day, Sunday, December 26. There are no weekdays before Epiphany, Epiphany is celebrated on Sunday, January 2, and there is a Monday through Saturday after Epiphany. The Baptism of the Lord is celebrated on Sunday, January 9.

### *Ordinary Time*

Ordinary Time derives its name from the word *ordinal*, meaning *number*. This season, therefore, is a season of weeks counted by numbers, from the First Week in Ordinary Time through the Thirty-Fourth Week in Ordinary Time. (Depending on the placement of Lent and Advent in any calendar year, Ordinary Time may end before the Thirty-Fourth Week.)

## Lent

The liturgical season of Lent lasts for 40 weekdays in remembrance of the 40 days and nights that Christ spent fasting in the desert, tempted by Satan. The beginning of Lent, Ash Wednesday, therefore comes 40 days (excluding Sundays) before Easter. Lent, in commemoration of Christ's fasting and prayer, is a time of fasting and prayer for all His faithful. Because of this austerity, *Alleluia* is not said in prayer or sung in liturgy during Lent.

## Easter

The season of Easter begins at the *Easter Vigil*.

But before that, the week previous to Easter is called Holy Week; it begins with Passion Sunday (Palm Sunday) and culminates with the *Triduum* (a Latin word for a three-day period) that begins with the Eve of Holy Thursday and concludes on Holy Saturday.

Easter is such a special time—it is the celebration of our Lord's resurrection, without which there would be no Christianity—that it continues not just for the week following Easter (the *Octave of Easter*—during which all days are celebrated as solemnities), but for 50 days (including Sundays and counting Easter Sunday itself) of the season of Easter.

The season of Easter comes to a close—and Ordinary Time returns—after Evening Prayer II of Pentecost.

Our Lord Jesus Christ told us to pray constantly (Luke 18:1). The Liturgy of the Hours provides one way to fulfill this obligation in a structured format. But, for the laity especially, without clear and unambiguous instructions, praying the Liturgy of the Hours can seem to be confusing and difficult.

Actually, everything anyone needs to learn the format of the Liturgy of the Hours can be found in the volumes themselves.

- The *General Instruction of the Liturgy of the Hours* (GILH) can be found in Volume I of the four-volume set.

- The section called the *Ordinary* in each volume provides complete instructions for the entire office.

"Digesting" all this information, however, can be difficult for someone without a liturgical background, and this fact alone can prevent many persons from learning a beautiful form of Catholic prayer.

Therefore, in the present book I have organized all the information you will need to learn to pray the Liturgy of the Hours using the four-volume set, step-by-step, as simply as possible. The single-volume *Christian Prayer* follows the same basic format as the four-volume set but omits Daytime Prayer and simplifies Night Prayer.

Everything is really much more simple than it seems. Most of the material in this present book is commentary meant to help you understand why and how you must do the "page flipping." But once you have "walked through it" a few times and catch on to the basic concepts you will find yourself moving through the Hours with ease and confidence.

📖 It will be helpful to use the *Saint Joseph Guide for the Liturgy of the Hours* (hereafter referred to as SJG), a small booklet that serves the entire calendar year. This booklet provides page references for each of the prayer times of every day. The SJG should be available in any Catholic bookstore, or you may buy it through the Internet. It's available for both the four-volume set and the one-volume Christian Prayer, so be careful to choose the correct booklet for your needs.

Each volume of the Liturgy of the Hours has several basic sections.

- The *Proper of Seasons* is found at the beginning of each volume. The *Proper of Seasons* follows a one-year cycle that begins with Advent and progresses through Christmas, Ordinary Time, Lent, Easter, and a second period of Ordinary Time; the material in each volume is specific to the time of year to which each volume is dedicated.

- The *Ordinary* contains general instructions for procedures to follow in each celebration: the Invitatory, the Office of Readings, Morning Prayer, Daytime Prayer, Evening Prayer, and Night Prayer.

- The *Psalter* contains the psalms (and, during Ordinary Time, the readings, intercessions, and prayers) for the Office of Readings, Morning Prayer, Daytime Prayer, and Evening Prayer. It follows a four-week cycle (i.e., Week I, Week II, Week III, and Week IV).

ⓘ To determine which Psalter week to use for any particular weekday, look in the Proper of Seasons for the Sunday which preceeds that day; a notation will indicate the Psalter week (for example, "Psalter, Week I") of that Sunday and, by implication, the weekdays that follow it.

• *Night Prayer* follows a simple daily cycle through the week; it does not vary during the liturgical seasons.

• The *Proper of Saints* contains material "proper" to (that is, specifically relating to) celebrations of various memorials, feasts, and solemnities throughout the year.

• The *Common of Saints* contains material common to celebrations of various kinds of saints: the Blessed Virgin, apostles, martyrs, pastors, virgins, and so on.

ⓘ Locate each section of your volume and place a ribbon there to mark the place for daily reference. Keep the ribbons for the *Ordinary* and for the *Night Prayer* sections fixed at the beginning of these respective sections because, when we need to go to those sections, we always start at the beginning of them; move the ribbons for the other

sections page-by-page as you progress through
each day of prayer.

## The Liturgy of the Hours has been designed to be sung.

- Nevertheless, the words *recited*, *said*, and *sung* can be interchanged, and it is allowable, especially in individual recitation, to simply "recite" the hours, as per the *General Instruction of the Liturgy of the Hours* (see GILH 267).

  ⓘ  Even the hymns can be recited, rather than sung, but because they "nourish prayer" they should not be omitted even in individual recitation (see GILH 280).

## Various postures may be used during the Office.

- In public recitation, everyone *stands* (a) during the introductory verses of each Hour; (b) during the hymn; (c) during the Gospel Canticle; and (d) during the intercessions, the Lord's Prayer, and the concluding prayer (see GILH 263).

- "All should *sit* to listen to the readings" (GILH 264). (Note that all should stand, however, for a Gospel reading used at an extended vigil; see GILH 73 and GILH 264.)

- "While the psalms and other canticles (with their antiphons) are being said, the assembly either sits or stands according to custom" (GILH 265).

- In individual, private recitation you may use whatever posture(s) you prefer, including sitting through the entire Office.

**Languages to be used during the Office.**

- Different languages may be used for various parts at one and the same celebration (see GILH 276). For example, parts readily known or available in Latin may be sung or recited in Latin during a celebration that is otherwise said in English. Parts especially suitable for this purpose would be (a) the hymn *Te Deum* (referred to by its first words in Latin), recited at the Office of Readings on Sundays, Solemnities, and Feasts; (b) the Canticle of Zechariah (also called the *Benedictus* from the first word in Latin), recited at Morning Prayer; (c) the Canticle of Mary (also called the *Magnificat* from the first word in Latin), recited at Evening Prayer; and (d) the Lord's Prayer (also called the *Pater Noster* from the first words in Latin).

**The Sign of the Cross is made at various times during the Office.**

- "All make the sign of the cross, from forehead to breast and from left shoulder to right shoulder (a) at the beginning of the Hours, when *God, come to my assistance* is being said; and (b) at the beginning of the Gospel Canticles of Zechariah, of Mary, and of Simeon" (GILH 266).

- "The sign of the cross is made on the mouth" with the side of the right thumb "at the beginning of the invitatory, at the words *Lord, open my lips*" (GILH 266).

- It would be appropriate for the sign of the cross to be made at the dismissal (or the final blessing), but the GILH does not say anything specific about this.

**Signs of reverence are made during the Office.**

- A bow of the head is made when the three Divine Persons are named (e.g., *Glory to the Father, and to the Son, and to the Holy Spirit* . . .), at the name of Jesus, at the name of Mary, and at the name of the Saint in whose honor the Liturgy of the Hours is celebrated. (See the *Ceremonial of Bishops*, 68; *General Instruction of the Roman Missal*, 275).

Throughout the Liturgy of the Hours, every psalm and canticle is concluded with the *Glory to the Father* unless otherwise indicated.

- Glory to the Father, and to the Son, and to the Holy Spirit: as it was in the beginning, is now, and will be for ever. Amen.

  (i) Notice that the format of the *Glory to the Father* used in the English translation of the Liturgy of the Hours is unique to this Office. This translation differs from the traditional English version (*Glory be to the Father, and to the Son, and to the Holy Spirit. As it was in the beginning, is now, and ever shall be, world without end. Amen.*) used in other liturgical services and in private devotion.

- The recitation of each psalm (or canticle) takes this order: antiphon, psalm, *Glory to the Father*, and antiphon. The psalm-prayer, which is optional, is said at the end of the psalm, after the *Glory to the Father* but before the concluding repetition of the antiphon. Alternatively, the psalm-prayer may follow an interval of silence after the repetition of the antiphon at the end of the psalm (see GILH 202).

In private recitation, the Office may take a contemplative quality.

- "In individual recitation there is greater freedom to pause in meditation on some text that moves the spirit, and the Office does not on this account lose its public character" (GILH 203). Thus you could not only pause to contemplate the meaning of a text, but you could also re-read the text more than once, taking as much time as suits you.

- In individual recitation not done under vows, you don't have to do everything "by the book." For example, if work obligations prevent you from saying an Hour at its proper time, you can say it at any other time; even if you make mistakes or forget something, you're still praying.

### The Office of Readings.

- The Office of Readings takes its traditional character as a night office of praise (see GILH 57). In fact, it may be recited "even during the night hours of the previous day, after Evening Prayer has been said" (GILH 59). Nevertheless, the Office of Readings "may be recited at any hour of the day" (GILH 59), and many persons, especially in individual recitation, prefer to celebrate the Office of Readings in the morning, immediately before Morning Prayer. That preference will be followed in this present book.

## 4   IN GENERAL

We will begin with those days on which no solemnities, feasts, or obligatory memorials are celebrated. These days all follow the same basic format.

(i)  Sundays are always celebrated as solemnities.

*Remember: At the beginning of each day, check the day's calendar date with the Proper of Saints; if the day is not a special celebration, then leave the ribbon between the last celebration and the next, for future use. Then orient yourself to the day's location in both the Psalter and the Proper of Seasons.*

# 5   THE INVITATORY

The invitatory consists of an antiphon specific to the day and one psalm. The Invitatory starts each day of prayer and is found at the very beginning of the Ordinary. Keep a ribbon permanently at that place because you will begin here every morning.

The invitatory begins as follows:

> Lord, open my lips.
> —And my mouth will proclaim your praise.

> *(Make the sign of the cross on your lips with the side of your thumb as you say these words, per GILH 266.)*

Then Psalm 95 (or, if you prefer, Psalm 100, 67, or 24) and its antiphon follows.

☑ In Ordinary Time, the antiphon is taken from the current weekday of the Psalter.

☑ Outside of Ordinary Time (i.e., during Advent, Christmas, Lent, and Easter), the antiphon will be given in the Ordinary according to the calendar dates within that season. To remind you of this, in the Psalter you will see the rubric, "Antiphon, as in the Ordinary."

After "Lord, open my lips . . . " is said, the antiphon is recited and immediately *repeated*. Then the first strophe of the psalm is said, then the antiphon is said, then the next strophe of the psalm is said, then the antiphon is said, and so on. Then the *Glory to the Father* is said, and then the antiphon is recited again to conclude.

ⓘ As indicated in the Ordinary, in individual recitation the antiphon need not be said after each strophe of the psalm; that is, the antiphon can be said only at the beginning of the psalm and following the *Glory to the Father*.

# 6    THE OFFICE OF READINGS

ⓘ The Office of Readings "may be recited at any hour
of the day" (GILH 59); many persons, especially in
individual recitation, prefer to celebrate the Office
of Readings in the morning, immediately before
Morning Prayer. That preference will be followed
in this present book.

## *Ordinary Time*

The hymn, antiphons, psalmody, and verse are found
in the Psalter.

ⓘ Preferably, the hymn should be sung, but, as circumstances require, and in individual recitation,
it may be recited.

ⓘ When the Office of Readings comes immediately
before Morning Prayer, the hymn designated for
the latter may be used in place of the hymn at the
beginning of the Office of Readings (see GILH 99).

📖 Notice how SJG says, "ALL" plus a number referring to the appropriate page of the Psalter, to
indicate that these initial parts of the Office come
from the Psalter.

A rubric in the Psalter will remind you that the readings
and prayer are "as in the Office of the day," and so they
are found in the Proper of Seasons.

📖 Notice how SJG says "Rd & Pr" plus a number referring to the appropriate page of the Proper of
Seasons.

ⓘ When Morning Prayer follows immediately, the
prayer and acclamation at the end of the Office of
Readings are not used (see GILH 99).

### Outside Ordinary Time

Outside Ordinary Time, the hymn should be tak-
en from a choice of hymns (as found in the Proper of
Seasons) that are appropriate to the season; the antiphons and psalmody are found in the Psalter. The verse,
readings and prayer are found in the Proper of Seasons;
a rubric in the Psalter will remind you of this by saying,
"Verse, readings and prayer, as in the Office of the day."

☑ Although you will find a hymn in the Psalter, it is

fitting that the hymn should come from the appropriate season.

ⓘ Preferably, the hymn should be sung, but, as circumstances require, and in individual recitation, it may be recited.

ⓘ When the Office of Readings comes immediately before Morning Prayer, the hymn designated for the latter may be used in place of the hymn at the beginning of the Office of Readings (see GILH 99).

📖 In Advent, SJG says, "ALL" plus a number referring to the appropriate page of the Psalter, from which the antiphons and psalmody come, and then "Ant, Rd, etc." plus a number referring to the appropriate page of the Proper of Seasons, from which the remainder of the Office is taken.

📖 In Lent and Easter, SJG says, "ALL" plus a number referring to the appropriate page of the Proper of Seasons, from which most of the Office comes, and then "Ps" plus a number referring to the appropriate page of the Psalter, from which the antiphons and psalmody are taken.

ⓘ When Morning Prayer follows immediately, the prayer and acclamation at the end of the Office of Readings are not used (see GILH 99).

# 7   MORNING PRAYER

Morning Prayer begins as follows, making *the sign of the cross* (from forehead to breast and from left shoulder to right shoulder) at the words, "God, come to my assistance," and *bowing the head* during the words, "Glory to the Father, and to the Son, and to the Holy Spirit":

God, come to my assistance.
—Lord, make haste to help me.
Glory to the Father, and to the Son, and to the
    Holy Spirit:
as it was in the beginning, is now, and will be
    forever. Amen. (Alleluia.)

ⓘ  When Morning Prayer follows immediately after the Office of Readings, the introductory *God, come to my assistance* and the *Glory to the Father* are omitted, as per the Ordinary.

ⓘ  For musical purposes, the invocation "God" may be expanded, for example, "O God," etc., as per

the Ordinary.

☑ *Alleluia* is omitted during Lent.

## *Ordinary Time*

The hymn is given in the Psalter. (It is omitted if the hymn for Morning Prayer was sung at the beginning of the Office of Readings immediately prior to Morning Prayer.)

The antiphons, psalmody, reading, responsory, antiphon for the Canticle of Zechariah, intercessions, and prayer are all found in the Psalter.

📖 SJG will say, "ALL" plus a number, to direct you to the beginning page of the Office in the Psalter.

ⓘ The sign of the cross is made at the beginning of the Canticle of Zechariah, and the canticle concludes with *Glory to the Father*.

In the absence of a priest or deacon, the conclusion (as found in the Ordinary) is as follows:

May the Lord bless us, protect us from all evil and bring us to everlasting life.
—Amen.

## *Outside Ordinary Time*

The hymn should be chosen from hymns appropriate to the season, as found in the Proper of Seasons. (The hymn is omitted if the hymn for Morning Prayer was sung at the beginning of the Office of Readings immediately prior to Morning Prayer.)

The antiphons and psalmody are found in the Psalter. A note in the Psalter will remind you that the reading, responsory, antiphon for the Canticle of Zechariah, intercessions, and prayer are "as in the Office of the day," and so they are found in the Proper of Seasons.

📖 In Advent, SJG will say, "ALL" plus a number, to direct you to the beginning page of the Office in the Psalter, and "Ant, Rd, etc." plus a number, to direct you to the beginning page of the Office in the Proper of Seasons.

📖 In Lent and Easter, SJG will say, "ALL" plus a number, to direct you to the beginning page of the Office in the Proper of Seasons, and "Ps" plus a number to direct you to the beginning page of the Office in the Psalter.

ⓘ The sign of the cross is made at the beginning of the Canticle of Zechariah, and the canticle concludes with *Glory to the Father*.

In the absence of a priest or deacon to give a blessing and the dismissal, or in individual recitation, the conclusion (as found in the Ordinary) is as follows:

May the Lord bless us, protect us from all evil and bring us to everlasting life.
—Amen.

# 8    DAYTIME PRAYER

ⓘ Religious who practice the contemplative life may
be required to recite all three Hours of Daytime
Prayer in choir, but in private recitation "it is permitted to choose from the three Hours the one
most appropriate to the time of day" (GILH 77). If
it is desired to recite all three Hours, a section of
Complimentary Psalmody can be found in each
volume between Night Prayer and the Proper of
Saints.

Daytime Prayer begins as follows, making *the sign of
the cross* (from forehead to breast and from left shoulder
to right shoulder) at the words, "God, come to my assistance," and *bowing the head* during the words, "Glory
to the Father, and to the Son, and to the Holy Spirit":

God, come to my assistance.
—Lord, make haste to help me.
Glory to the Father, and to the Son, and to the
    Holy Spirit:
as it was in the beginning, is now, and will be

forever. Amen. (Alleluia.)

ⓘ  For musical purposes, the invocation "God" may
   be expanded, for example, "O God," etc., as per
   the Ordinary.

☑  *Alleluia* is omitted during Lent.

### Ordinary Time

The hymn is found in the Ordinary. Everything else is
found in the Psalter, unless you are praying an additional Hour or two that requires the Complimentary
Psalmody.

📖  In Ordinary Time, SJG will say, "ALL" plus a number,
   to direct you to the beginning page of the Office
   in the Psalter, and "Rd & Pr" to direct you to the
   beginning page of the Office in the Proper of
   Seasons.

### Outside Ordinary Time

The hymn is found in the Ordinary. The antiphon
comes from the Proper of Seasons (a note in the Psalter
will remind you of this), the psalmody comes from the
Psalter (unless you are praying an additional Hour or

two that requires the Complimentary Psalmody), and the reading, verse, and prayer come from the Proper of Seasons (a note in the Psalter will say, "Reading, verse, and prayer, as in the Office of the day").

📖 In Advent and the Christmas season, SJG will say, "ALL" plus a number, to direct you to the beginning page of the Office in the Psalter, and "Ant, Rd, etc." plus a number, to direct you to the beginning page of the Office in the Proper of Seasons.

📖 In Lent and Easter, SJG will say, "ALL" plus a number, to direct you to the beginning page of the Office in the Proper of Seasons, and "Ps" plus a number to direct you to the beginning page of the Office in the Psalter.

In Ordinary Time and outside Ordinary Time, the conclusion (as found in the Ordinary) is as follows:

Let us praise the Lord.
—And give Him thanks.

# 9    EVENING PRAYER

☑ If a solemnity follows the current day, then Evening Prayer I of the solemnity is celebrated, not the Evening Prayer II of the current regular day. Sundays are always celebrated as solemnities, so Evening Prayer on regular Saturdays will be Evening Prayer I of the following Sunday.

Evening Prayer begins as follows, making *the sign of the cross* (from forehead to breast and from left shoulder to right shoulder) at the words, "God, come to my assistance," and *bowing the head* during the words, "Glory to the Father, and to the Son, and to the Holy Spirit":

God, come to my assistance.
—Lord, make haste to help me.
Glory to the Father, and to the Son, and to the
    Holy Spirit:
as it was in the beginning, is now, and will be
    forever. Amen. (Alleluia.)

ⓘ For musical purposes, the invocation "God" may

be expanded, for example, "O God," etc., as per the Ordinary.

☑ *Alleluia* is omitted during Lent.

## Ordinary Time

The hymn, antiphons, psalmody, reading, responsory, antiphon for the Canticle of Mary, intercessions, and prayer are all found in the Psalter.

📖 SJG will say, "ALL" plus a number, to direct you to the beginning page of the Office in the Psalter.

ⓘ The sign of the cross is made at the beginning of the Canticle of Mary, and the canticle concludes with *Glory to the Father*.

## Outside Ordinary Time

The hymn should be chosen from hymns appropriate to the season, as found in the Proper of Seasons.

The antiphons and psalmody are found in the Psalter. A note in the Psalter will remind you that the reading, responsory, antiphon for the Canticle of Mary, intercessions, and prayer are "as in the Office of the day," and so they are found in the Proper of Seasons.

📖 In Lent and Easter, SJG will say, "ALL" plus a number, to direct you to the beginning page of the Office in the Proper of Seasons, and "Ps" plus a number to direct you to the beginning page of the Office in the Psalter. In Advent, SJG will say, "ALL" plus a number, to direct you to the beginning page of the Office in the Psalter, and "Ant, Rd, etc." plus a number, to direct you to the beginning page of the Office in the Proper of Seasons.

ⓘ The sign of the cross is made at the beginning of the Canticle of Mary, and the canticle concludes with *Glory to the Father*.

The conclusion of the Hour is the same whether during Ordinary Time or outside Ordinary Time. In the absence of a priest or deacon to give a blessing and the dismissal, or in individual recitation, the conclusion (as found in the Ordinary) is as follows:

May the Lord bless us, protect us from all evil and bring us to everlasting life.
—Amen.

## 10  NIGHT PRAYER

You may find it helpful to have a permanent ribbon marking the beginning of this section because Night Prayer always begins at the same place.

Night Prayer begins as follows, making *the sign of the cross* (from forehead to breast and from left shoulder to right shoulder) at the words, "God, come to my assistance," and *bowing the head* during the words, "Glory to the Father, and to the Son, and to the Holy Spirit":

God, come to my assistance.
—Lord, make haste to help me.
Glory to the Father, and to the Son, and to the
    Holy Spirit:
as it was in the beginning, is now, and will be
    forever. Amen. (Alleluia.)

ⓘ  For musical purposes, the invocation "God" may be expanded; for example, "O God," etc., as per the Ordinary.

☑   *Alleluia* is omitted during Lent.

Then a brief examination of conscience may be made as you review the events of the day.

Everything else is found in the Night Prayer section for the current the day of the week.

ⓘ   If the following day is a solemnity, use the section of Night Prayer called "After Evening Prayer I on Sundays and Solemnities".

📖   SJG will say, "NP" plus a number, to direct you to the appropriate page of the Night Prayer.

☑   During *Lent*, the alleluias at the end of each verse of the responsory are not said.

During the *Easter Triduum*, in place of the responsory, the antiphon "For our sake Christ was obedient, accepting even death [etc. as per the day]" is said.

During the *Octave of Easter*, in place of the responsory, the following antiphon is said: "This is the day the Lord has made; let us rejoice and be glad, alleluia."

ⓘ   The sign of the cross is made at the beginning of

the Gospel canticle, and the canticle concludes
with *Glory to the Father.*

The conclusion for Night Prayer is as follows:

May the all-powerful Lord grant us a restful
   night and a peaceful death.
—Amen.

Then one of the antiphons in honor of the Blessed
Virgin Mary is said; these antiphons are found at the
very end of the Night Prayer section.

- The *Alma Redemptoris Mater* (Loving Mother of
  the Redeemer) is traditionally recited from the First
  Sunday of Advent to the Feast of the Presentation.

- The *Ave Regina Cœlorum* (Hail, Queen of the
  Heavens) is traditionally recited from after the
  Presentation to Holy Saturday.

- The *Regina Cœli* (Queen of Heaven) is traditionally
  recited from Easter Sunday to Pentecost Sunday.

- The *Salve Regina* (Hail, Holy Queen) is traditionally
  recited from after Pentecost until the First Sunday
  of Advent.

# 11   GRAPHIC SUMMARY: GENERAL

### INVITATORY
#### *General*

| Proper of Seasons | Ordinary | Psalter | Proper of Saints | Commons |
|---|---|---|---|---|
|  |  | Antiphon. |  |  |
|  | Psalm. |  |  |  |

### INVITATORY
#### *General—Outside Ordinary Time*

| Proper of Seasons | Ordinary | Psalter | Proper of Saints | Commons |
|---|---|---|---|---|
|  | Antiphon and psalm. |  |  |  |

## OFFICE OF READINGS
### *General*

| Proper of Seasons | Ordinary | Psalter | Proper of Saints | Commons |
|---|---|---|---|---|
| | | Hymn, antiphons, psalmody, and verse. | | |
| Readings and prayer. | | | | |

## OFFICE OF READINGS
### *General—Outside Ordinary Time*

| Proper of Seasons | Ordinary | Psalter | Proper of Saints | Commons |
|---|---|---|---|---|
| | | Hymn, antiphons, and psalmody. | | |
| Verse, readings, and prayer. | | | | |

## Morning Prayer
### General

| Proper of Seasons | Ordinary | Psalter | Proper of Saints | Commons |
|---|---|---|---|---|
| | | Hymn, antiphons, psalmody, reading, responsory, antiphon for the Canticle of Zechariah, intercessions, and prayer. | | |

## Morning Prayer
### General—Outside Ordinary Time

| Ordinary | Proper of Seasons | Psalter | Proper of Saints | Commons |
|---|---|---|---|---|
| | Hymn. | | | |
| | | Antiphons and psalmody. | | |
| | Reading, responsory, antiphon for the Canticle of Zechariah, intercessions, and prayer. | | | |

## Daytime Prayer
### *General*

| Proper of Seasons | Ordinary | Psalter | Proper of Saints | Commons |
|---|---|---|---|---|
|  | Hymn. |  |  |  |
|  |  | Antiphons, psalmody, reading, verse, and prayer. |  |  |

## Daytime Prayer
### *General—Outside Ordinary Time*

| Proper of Seasons | Ordinary | Psalter | Proper of Saints | Commons |
|---|---|---|---|---|
| Hymn. | | |  |  |
| Antiphon. |  |  |  |  |
|  |  | Psalmody. |  |  |
| Reading, verse, and prayer. |  |  |  |  |

## Evening Prayer
### *General*

| Proper of Seasons | Ordinary | Psalter | Proper of Saints | Commons |
|---|---|---|---|---|
| | | Hymn, antiphons, psalmody, reading, responsory, antiphon for the Canticle of Mary, intercessions, and prayer. | | |

## Evening Prayer
### *General—Outside Ordinary Time*

| Ordinary | Proper of Seasons | Psalter | Proper of Saints | Commons |
|---|---|---|---|---|
| | Hymn. | | | |
| | | Antiphons and psalmody. | | |
| | Reading, responsory, antiphon for the Canticle of Mary, intercessions, and prayer. | | | |

## 12  MEMORIALS

There are two kinds of memorials: *obligatory memorials* and *optional memorials.* In most circumstances, the obligatory memorials must be celebrated, but the optional memorials can be celebrated or not according to preference.

(i) Some days have more than one optional memorial. It is purely a matter of preference which memorial, if any, is celebrated.

📖 Optional memorials are indicated in the SJG by listing first the current day followed by an "OR:" with the listing for the optional memorial(s).

☑ Sundays are always celebrated as solemnities, and because all solemnities take liturgical precedence over memorials, any memorial that occurs on a Sunday is disregarded.

☑ Memorials are not celebrated during Lent. Saints

whose days occur during the time of Lent are remembered with optional *commemorations* which allow the use of the second reading and the prayer from the Proper of Saints. The SJG will say, "May add Rd & Pr of St. N etc." along with the relevant page numbers. (Memorials that occur during Holy Week are disregarded.)

In the following chapters on Memorials, the Presentation of Mary, November 21, from Volume IV, will be used as an example of praying the Liturgy of the Hours on memorials.

*Remember: At the beginning of each day, check the day in the SJG, and orient yourself to the day's location in both the Psalter and the Proper of Seasons. If the day is a memorial, put a ribbon in the Proper of Saints for the rest of the day's prayer. Also, place a ribbon in the appropriate section of the Commons—the Proper of Saints will tell you which Common to use.*

# 13 THE INVITATORY
## ON MEMORIALS

☑ Memorials are not celebrated during Lent. Saints whose days occur during the time of Lent are remembered with optional *commemorations* which allow the use of the second reading and the prayer from the Proper of Saints. The SJG will say, "May add Rd & Pr of St. N etc." along with the relevant page numbers. (Memorials that occur during Holy Week are disregarded.)

The invitatory belongs at the beginning of each day of prayer, so you may find it helpful to have a ribbon permanently at its place in the Ordinary.

The invitatory begins as follows:

Lord, open my lips.
—And my mouth will proclaim your praise.

*(Make the sign of the cross on your lips with the side of your thumb as you say these words, per GILH*

*266.)*

Then Psalm 95 (or, if you prefer, Psalm 100, 67, or 24) and its antiphon follows. The antiphon is taken from the Commons (or the weekday, if you prefer), unless it is given in the Proper of Saints.

> 📖 As an example from the Presentation of Mary, November 21, from Volume IV, the antiphon can be found in the Common of the Blessed Virgin Mary, on page 1628. Notice how SJG says "Com of BVM 1628" to indicate this.

After "Lord, open my lips . . . " is said, the antiphon is recited and immediately *repeated*. Then the first strophe of the psalm is said, then the antiphon is said, then the next strophe of the psalm is said, then the antiphon is said, and so on. Then the *Glory to the Father* is said, and then the antiphon is recited again to conclude.

> ⓘ As indicated in the Ordinary, in individual recitation the antiphon need not be said after each strophe of the psalm; that is, the antiphon can be said only at the beginning of the psalm and following the *Glory to the Father*.

# 14 THE OFFICE OF READINGS ON MEMORIALS

☑ Memorials are not celebrated during Lent. Saints whose days occur during the time of Lent are remembered with optional *commemorations* which allow the use of the second reading and the prayer from the Proper of Saints. The SJG will say, "May add Rd & Pr of St. N etc." along with the relevant page numbers. (Memorials that occur during Holy Week are disregarded.)

ⓘ The Office of Readings "may be recited at any hour of the day" (GILH 59); many persons, especially in individual recitation, prefer to celebrate the Office of Readings in the morning, immediately before Morning Prayer. That preference will be followed in this present book.

The hymn is taken from the Commons (or the weekday, if you prefer), unless it is given in the Proper of Saints.

📖 As an example from the Presentation of Mary,

November 21, from Volume IV, the hymn can be found in the Common of the Blessed Virgin Mary, on page 1628. Notice how SJG says, "From Com of BVM" plus a number referring to the appropriate page of the Commons.

(i) When the Office of Readings comes immediately before Morning Prayer, the hymn designated for the latter may be used in place of the hymn at the beginning of the Office of Readings (see GILH 99).

(i) Preferably, the hymn should be sung, but, as circumstances require, and in individual recitation, it may be recited.

**The psalmody, antiphons, and verse are found in the Psalter under the current weekday.**

📖 SJG will say, "OOR" plus a number, to direct you to the appropriate page of the Psalter.

☑ Notice how the Commons have psalms and antiphons for the Office of Readings. You must *disregard them all*, because the Ordinary says that on memorials "the psalms and antiphons are taken from the current week of the Psalter, unless there are proper psalms and antiphons."

📖 As an example from the Presentation of Mary,

November 21, from Volume IV, the psalms and antiphons are found in the Psalter according to the current weekday, which will vary year by year. Notice how SJG says "OOR [page varies]" to indicate this.

The first reading and responsory are taken from the Proper of Seasons according to the current weekday. Note that although there is also a second reading in the Proper of Seasons, the celebration of the Memorial requires that the second reading, its responsory, and the prayer all be taken from the Proper of Saints. (In individual recitation, though, you may read and meditate on both of the second readings if you want to do so.)

📖 As an example from the Presentation of Mary, November 21, from Volume IV, the first reading is found in the Proper of Seasons, but the weekday will vary year by year. The second reading is found on page 1572 of the Proper of Saints, and the prayer is found on page 1575 of the Proper of Saints. Notice how SJG says "Rd [page varies] & 1572" and "Pr 1575" to indicate this.

ⓘ When Morning Prayer follows immediately, the prayer and acclamation at the end of the Office of Readings are not used (see GILH 99).

## 15 MORNING PRAYER ON MEMORIALS

☑ Memorials are not celebrated during Lent. Saints whose days occur during the time of Lent are remembered with optional *commemorations* which allow the use of the second reading and the prayer from the Proper of Saints. The SJG will say, "May add Rd & Pr of St. N etc." along with the relevant page numbers. (Memorials that occur during Holy Week are disregarded.)

Morning Prayer begins as follows, making *the sign of the cross* (from forehead to breast and from left shoulder to right shoulder) at the words, "God, come to my assistance," and *bowing the head* during the words, "Glory to the Father, and to the Son, and to the Holy Spirit":

God, come to my assistance.
—Lord, make haste to help me.
Glory to the Father, and to the Son, and to the
    Holy Spirit:
as it was in the beginning, is now, and will be

forever. Amen. (Alleluia.)

ⓘ When Morning Prayer follows immediately after the Office of Readings, the introductory *God, come to my assistance* and the *Glory to the Father* are omitted, as per the Ordinary.

ⓘ For musical purposes, the invocation "God" may be expanded, for example, "O God," etc., as per the Ordinary.

The hymn is taken from the Commons (or the weekday, if you prefer), unless it is given in the Proper of Saints. (The hymn is omitted if the hymn for Morning Prayer was sung at the beginning of the Office of Readings immediately prior to Morning Prayer.)

The psalmody and antiphons are usually taken from the Psalter. Sometimes, on rare occasions (for example, Martin of Tours, November 11, and Agnes, January 21) the psalmody and antiphons are given in the Proper of Saints.

📖 As an example from the Presentation of Mary, November 21, from Volume IV, the psalms and antiphons are found in the Psalter, but the weekday will vary year by year. Notice how SJG says "Ps" plus a number referring you to the appropriate page of the Psalter.

☑ Notice how the Commons have psalms and antiphons for Morning Prayer. You must *disregard
them all*, because the Ordinary says that on memorials "the psalms, canticle, and antiphons are
taken from the current week of the Psalter, unless
there are proper psalms and antiphons."

The reading, unless it is proper, may be taken from either the Commons or the weekday.

☑ There will be no clue in the Psalter that you have
the option to go to the Commons for the reading,
responsory, etc. of the remainder of the celebration, rather than just continue reading along in
the Psalter. This is why it is important to understand the rules for the Liturgy of the Hours and
react to them automatically.

The antiphon for the Canticle of Zechariah is taken
from the Commons, unless there is a proper antiphon.

The intercessions, unless they are proper, may be taken
from either the Commons or the weekday.

The concluding prayer is taken from the Proper of
Saints.

📖 As an example from the Presentation of Mary,
November 21, from Volume IV, the reading,

responsory, and intercessions are found in the Common of the Blessed Virgin Mary, beginning on page 1640, and the Canticle of Zechariah and the prayer are given in the Proper of Saints, page 1575. Notice how SJG says, "MP" plus a number referring to the appropriate page of the Commons, and "Ant & Pr" plus a number referring to the appropriate page of the Proper of Saints.

ⓘ The sign of the cross is made at the beginning of the Canticle of Zechariah, and the canticle concludes with *Glory to the Father*.

In the absence of a priest or deacon to give a blessing and the dismissal, or in individual recitation, the conclusion (as found in the Ordinary) is as follows:

May the Lord bless us, protect us from all evil, and bring us to everlasting life.
—Amen.

# 16 DAYTIME PRAYER ON MEMORIALS

☑ Memorials are not celebrated during Lent. Saints whose days occur during the time of Lent are remembered with optional *commemorations* which allow the use of the second reading and the prayer from the Proper of Saints. The SJG will say, "May add Rd & Pr of St. N etc." along with the relevant page numbers. (Memorials that occur during Holy Week are disregarded.)

☑ The memorials of saints are not ever celebrated at Daytime Prayer, so Daytime Prayer is celebrated as an ordinary weekday, according to its current season—unless the Proper of Saints indicates otherwise.

ⓘ Religious who practice the contemplative life may be required to recite all three Hours of Daytime Prayer in choir, but in private recitation "it is permitted to choose from the three Hours the one most appropriate to the time of day" (GILH 77). If it is desired to recite all three Hours, a section of Complimentary Psalmody can be found in each volume between Night Prayer and the Proper of Saints.

Daytime Prayer begins as follows, making *the sign of the cross* (from forehead to breast and from left shoulder to right shoulder) at the words, "God, come to my assistance," and *bowing the head* during the words, "Glory to the Father, and to the Son, and to the Holy Spirit":

God, come to my assistance.
—Lord, make haste to help me.
Glory to the Father, and to the Son, and to the
   Holy Spirit:
as it was in the beginning, is now, and will be
   forever. Amen. (Alleluia.)

ⓘ   For musical purposes, the invocation "God" may be expanded, for example, "O God," etc., as per the Ordinary.

The hymn is found in the Ordinary. Everything else is found in the Psalter during Ordinary Time. Outside Ordinary Time, and unless the Proper of Saints directs you otherwise, the antiphon comes from the Proper of Seasons (a note in the Psalter will remind you of this), the psalmody comes from the Psalter, and the reading, verse, and prayer come from the Proper of Seasons (a note in the Psalter will say, "Reading, verse, and prayer, as in the Office of the day").

📖 In Ordinary Time, SJG will say, "ALL" plus a number, to direct you to the beginning page of the Office in the Psalter, and "Rd & Pr" to direct you to the beginning page of the Office in the Proper of Seasons.

📖 In Advent and the Christmas season, SJG will say, "ALL" plus a number, to direct you to the beginning page of the Office in the Psalter, and "Ant, Rd, etc." plus a number, to direct you to the beginning page of the Office in the Proper of Seasons.

📖 In the season of Easter, SJG will say, "ALL" plus a number, to direct you to the beginning page of the Office in the Proper of Seasons, and "Ps" plus a number to direct you to the beginning page of the Office in the Psalter.

The conclusion (as found in the Ordinary) is as follows:

Let us praise the Lord.
—And give Him thanks.

## 17  EVENING PRAYER ON MEMORIALS

☑ Memorials are not celebrated during Lent. Saints whose days occur during the time of Lent are remembered with optional *commemorations* which allow the use of the second reading and the prayer from the Proper of Saints. The SJG will say, "May add Rd & Pr of St. N etc." along with the relevant page numbers. (Memorials that occur during Holy Week are disregarded.)

ⓘ If a solemnity follows the current day, then Evening Prayer I of the solemnity is celebrated, not Evening Prayer II of the current memorial. Sundays are always celebrated as solemnities, so Evening Prayer on Saturday memorials will be Evening Prayer I of the following Sunday.

Evening Prayer begins as follows, making *the sign of the cross* (from forehead to breast and from left shoulder to right shoulder) at the words, "God, come to my assistance," and *bowing the head* during the words, "Glory to the Father, and to the Son, and to the Holy Spirit":

> God, come to my assistance.
> —Lord, make haste to help me.
> Glory to the Father, and to the Son, and to the
>     Holy Spirit:
> as it was in the beginning, is now, and will be
>     forever. Amen. (Alleluia.)

> ⓘ  For musical purposes, the invocation "God" may
> be expanded, for example, "O God," etc., as per
> the Ordinary.

The hymn is taken from the Commons (or the weekday, if you prefer), unless it is given in the Proper of Saints.

> 📖  As an example from the Presentation of Mary,
> November 21, from Volume IV, the hymn can be
> found in the Common of the Blessed Virgin Mary,
> on page 1648. Notice how SJG says, "EP 1648" plus
> a number referring to the appropriate page of the
> Commons.

The psalmody and antiphons are usually taken from the Psalter. Sometimes, on rare occasions (see Martin of Tours, November 11) the psalmody and antiphons are given in the Proper of Saints.

> 📖  As an example from the Presentation of Mary,

November 21, from Volume IV, the psalms and antiphons are found in the Psalter, according to the current day of the week; the actual weekday will vary year by year. Notice how SJG says "Ps" plus a number referring to the appropriate page of the Psalter.

☑ Notice how the Commons have psalms and antiphons for Evening Prayer. You must *disregard them all*, because the Ordinary says that on memorials "the psalms, canticle, and antiphons are taken from the current week of the Psalter, unless there are proper psalms and antiphons."

The reading, unless it is proper, may be taken from either the Commons or the weekday.

☑ There will be no clue in the Psalter that you have the option to go to the Commons for the reading, responsory, etc. of the remainder of the celebration, rather than just continue reading along in the Psalter. This is why it is important to understand the rules for the Liturgy of the Hours and react to them automatically.

The antiphon for the Canticle of Mary is taken from the Commons, unless there is a proper antiphon.

The intercessions, unless they are proper, may be taken

from either the Commons or the weekday.

The concluding prayer is taken from the Proper of Saints.

📖 As an example from the Presentation of Mary, November 21, from Volume IV, the reading, responsory, and intercessions are all found in the Common of the Blessed Virgin Mary, beginning on page 1648, and the antiphon for the Canticle of Mary and the prayer are given in the Proper of Saints, page 1575. Notice how SJG says "EP" plus a number referring to the appropriate page of the Commons, and "Ant & Pr" plus a number referring to the appropriate page of the Proper of Saints.

ⓘ The sign of the cross is made at the beginning of the Canticle of Mary, and the canticle concludes with *Glory to the Father*.

In the absence of a priest or deacon to give a blessing and the dismissal, or in individual recitation, the conclusion (as found in the Ordinary) is as follows:

May the Lord bless us, protect us from all evil, and bring us to everlasting life.
—Amen.

## 18 NIGHT PRAYER
## ON MEMORIALS

☑ Memorials are not celebrated during Lent. Saints
whose days occur during the time of Lent are
remembered with optional *commemorations*
which allow the use of the second reading and
the prayer from the Proper of Saints. The SJG will
say, "May add Rd & Pr of St. N etc." along with the
relevant page numbers. (Memorials that occur
during Holy Week are disregarded.)

You may find it helpful to have a permanent ribbon
marking the beginning of this section because Night
Prayer always begins at the same place.

Night Prayer begins as follows, making *the sign of the
cross* (from forehead to breast and from left shoulder to
right shoulder) at the words, "God, come to my assistance," and *bowing the head* during the words, "Glory to
the Father, and to the Son, and to the Holy Spirit":

God, come to my assistance.

—Lord, make haste to help me.

Glory to the Father, and to the Son, and to the
   Holy Spirit:

as it was in the beginning, is now, and will be
   forever. Amen. (Alleluia.)

(i) For musical purposes, the invocation "God" may
   be expanded; for example, "O God," etc., as per
   the Ordinary.

Then a brief examination of conscience may be made as
you review the events of the day.

Everything else is found in the Night Prayer section, according to the day of the week.

(i) If the following day is a solemnity, use the section
   of Night Prayer called "After Evening Prayer I on
   Sundays and Solemnities".

📖 SJG will say, "NP" plus a number, to direct you to
   the appropriate page of the Night Prayer.

☑ During *Lent*, the alleluias at the end of each verse
   of the responsory are not said.

   During the *Easter Triduum*, in place of the responsory, the antiphon "For our sake Christ was obedient, accepting even death [etc. as per the day]"

is said.

During the *Octave of Easter*, in place of the responsory, the following antiphon is said: "This is the day the Lord has made; let us rejoice and be glad, alleluia."

ⓘ The sign of the cross is made at the beginning of the Gospel canticle, and the canticle concludes with *Glory to the Father*.

The conclusion for Night Prayer is as follows:

May the all-powerful Lord grant us a restful night and a peaceful death.
—Amen.

Then one of the antiphons in honor of the Blessed Virgin Mary is said; these antiphons are found at the very end of the Night Prayer section.

• The *Alma Redemptoris Mater* (Loving Mother of the Redeemer) is traditionally recited from the First Sunday of Advent to the Feast of the Presentation.

• The *Ave Regina Cælorum* (Hail, Queen of the Heavens) is traditionally recited from after the

Presentation to Holy Saturday.

- The *Regina Cœli* (Queen of Heaven) is traditionally recited from Easter Sunday to Pentecost Sunday.

- The *Salve Regina* (Hail, Holy Queen) is traditionally recited from after Pentecost until the First Sunday of Advent.

# 19 GRAPHIC SUMMARY: MEMORIALS

## INVITATORY

### *Memorials*

| Proper of Seasons | Ordinary | Psalter | Proper of Saints | Commons |
|---|---|---|---|---|
| | | | Antiphon. (Use the Commons if not given in the Proper of Saints.) | |
| | Psalm. | | | |

## Office of Readings
### *Memorials*

| Proper of Seasons | Ordinary | Psalter | Proper of Saints | Commons |
|---|---|---|---|---|
| | | | Hymn.<br><br>(Use the Commons if not given in the Proper of Saints.) | |
| | | Psalmody, antiphons, and verse, unless given in the Proper of Saints. | | |
| First reading and responsory. | | | | |
| | | | Second reading, responsory, and prayer.<br><br>(Use the Commons if not given in the Proper of Saints.) | |

# Morning Prayer
## *Memorials*

| Proper of Seasons | Ordinary | Psalter | Proper of Saints | Commons |
|---|---|---|---|---|
| | | Hymn.<br><br>(Use the Commons or the weekday if not given in the Proper of Saints.) | | |
| | | Antiphons and psalmody.<br><br>(If given in the Proper of Saints, use those; otherwise use the Psalter.) | | |
| | | Reading, responsory, antiphon for the Canticle of Zechariah, intercessions, and prayer.<br><br>(If any of these are given in the Proper of Saints, use them; otherwise, any of these may be taken from the Commons or the weekday, as desired.) | | |

## Daytime Prayer
### *As in Ordinary Time*

| Proper of Seasons | Ordinary | Psalter | Proper of Saints | Commons |
|---|---|---|---|---|
| | Hymn. | | | |
| | | Antiphons, psalmody, reading, verse, and prayer. | | |

### *As outside Ordinary Time*

| Proper of Seasons | Ordinary | Psalter | Proper of Saints | Commons |
|---|---|---|---|---|
| Hymn. | | | | |
| Antiphon. | | | | |
| | | Psalmody. | | |
| Reading, verse, and prayer. | | | | |

## Evening Prayer
### *Memorials*

| Proper of Seasons | Ordinary | Psalter | Proper of Saints | Commons |
|---|---|---|---|---|
| | | Hymn.<br><br>(Use the Commons or the weekday if not given in the Proper of Saints.) | | |
| | | Antiphons and psalmody.<br><br>(If given in the Proper of Saints, use those; otherwise use the Psalter.) | | |
| | | Reading, responsory, antiphon for the Canticle of Mary, intercessions, and prayer.<br><br>(If any of these are given in the Proper of Saints, use them; otherwise, any of these may be taken from the Commons or the weekday, as desired.) | | |

# 20  FEASTS

All the Apostles' days are celebrated as feasts. In addition, some days of the Blessed Virgin and of Christ are celebrated as feasts. On some feasts, everything in the Office comes from the Proper of Saints; on other feasts, some parts come from the Proper of Saints and some from the Commons; and on one feast, the *Baptism of the Lord*, everything in the Office comes from the Proper of Seasons.

(i) Occasionally, a feast will occur on a Sunday. For example, on December 28, the *Holy Innocents, Martyrs* is celebrated as a feast, but if this feast occurs on a Sunday it can be preempted by the *Holy Family,* also a feast but of greater liturgical precedence than most other feasts. As another example, on December 12, *Our Lady of Guadalupe* is celebrated in the U.S. as a feast, but if this feast occurs on a Sunday it can be preempted by the Third Sunday of Advent, a Solemnity of Our Lord. In general, when a feast is impeded by (a)

another feast of greater liturgical precedence, or
(b) a solemnity, or (c) Holy Week, the feast is ig-
nored for that year—regardless of what popular
sentiment (and cultural pride) might desire.

Some feasts, such as the Baptism of the Lord, are
uncomplicated, because everything comes from the
Proper of Saints. In the following chapters about feasts,
the Birth of Mary, September 8, from Volume IV, will
be used as an example for praying the Liturgy of the
Hours on feasts.

*Remember: At the beginning of each day, check the day in
the SJG, and orient yourself to the day's location in both the
Psalter and the Proper of Seasons. If the day is a feast, put a
ribbon in the Proper of Saints so you will have it in place for
the rest of the day's prayer. Also, if the Proper of Saints tells
you to use the Commons, place a ribbon in the appropriate
section of the Commons for that day.*

## 21 THE INVITATORY
## ON FEASTS

The invitatory belongs at the beginning of each day of prayer, so you may find it helpful to have a ribbon permanently at its place in the Ordinary.

The invitatory begins as follows:

Lord, open my lips.
—And my mouth will proclaim your praise.

*(Make the sign of the cross on your lips with the side of your thumb as you say these words, per GILH 266.)*

Then Psalm 95 (or, if you prefer, Psalm 100, 67, or 24) and its antiphon follows.

The antiphon is taken from the Proper of Saints.

📖 Notice how SJG gives a number in parentheses on

the title line to indicate where to find the current day in the Proper of Saints.

After "Lord, open my lips . . . " is said, the antiphon is recited and immediately *repeated*. Then the first strophe of the psalm is said, then the antiphon is said, then the next strophe of the psalm is said, then the antiphon is said, and so on. Then the *Glory to the Father* is said, and then the antiphon is recited again to conclude.

ⓘ As indicated in the Ordinary, in individual recitation the antiphon need not be said after each strophe of the psalm; that is, the antiphon can be said only at the beginning of the psalm and following the *Glory to the Father*.

## 22 THE OFFICE OF READINGS ON FEASTS

ⓘ The Office of Readings "may be recited at any hour of the day" (GILH 59); many persons, especially in individual recitation, prefer to celebrate the Office of Readings in the morning, immediately before Morning Prayer. That preference will be followed in this present book.

The hymn, if not given in the Proper of Saints, is taken from the Commons *as specified in the Proper of Saints.*

ⓘ When the Office of Readings comes immediately before Morning Prayer, the hymn designated for the latter may be used in place of the hymn at the beginning of the Office of Readings (see GILH 99).

ⓘ Preferably, the hymn should be sung, but, as circumstances require, and in individual recitation, it may be recited.

The psalmody, antiphons, and verse, if not given in the

Proper of Saints, are taken from the Commons. (This is stated at the beginning of the Proper of Saints.

The first reading and responsory, if not given in the Proper of Saints, are taken from the Commons.

The second reading and responsory are given in the Proper of Saints.

☑ Outside of Ordinary Time, follow the instructions in the Proper of Saints. If a rubric says, for example, "From the Common of Apostles during the Easter Season, 1951, except for the following:" and if no first reading is given in the Proper of Saints, then take the first reading from the Common of Apostles.

The hymn *Te Deum* is said after the responsory for the second reading.

📖 Notice how SJG gives a number in parentheses on the title line to indicate where to find the current day in the Proper of Saints. And notice how SJG says, "Te Deum" to remind you about the *Te Deum*.

The prayer is given in the Proper of Saints.

ⓘ When Morning Prayer follows immediately, the

prayer and acclamation at the end of the Office of Readings are not used (see GILH 99).

As an example from the Birth of Mary, September 8, from Volume IV, the hymn, antiphons, psalms, and verse are all found in the Common of the Blessed Virgin Mary, beginning on page 1628; both readings and their responsories are found in the Proper of Saints; and the prayer is as in Morning Prayer. Notice how SJG says "From Com of BVM" plus a number referring to the appropriate page of the Commons, and "proper, Te Deum" telling you that everything else not in the Commons is specified in the Proper of Saints, while reminding you to say the *Te deum.*

## 23 MORNING PRAYER ON FEASTS

Morning Prayer begins as follows, making *the sign of the cross* (from forehead to breast and from left shoulder to right shoulder) at the words, "God, come to my assistance," and *bowing the head* during the words, "Glory to the Father, and to the Son, and to the Holy Spirit":

God, come to my assistance.
—Lord, make haste to help me.
Glory to the Father, and to the Son, and to the Holy Spirit:
as it was in the beginning, is now, and will be forever. Amen. (Alleluia.)

ⓘ When Morning Prayer follows immediately after the Office of Readings, the introductory *God, come to my assistance* and the *Glory to the Father* are omitted, as per the Ordinary.

ⓘ For musical purposes, the invocation "God" may

be expanded, for example, "O God," etc., as per the Ordinary.

☑ *Alleluia* is omitted during Lent.

If the hymn is not given in the Proper of Saints, you will be referred to the Common of Saints. (The hymn is omitted here if a hymn was sung at the beginning of the Office of Readings immediately prior to Morning Prayer.)

The antiphons, if not given in the Proper of Saints, are taken from the Commons, with directions to use the psalms and canticle from Sunday of Week I.

📖 Notice how SJG gives a number in parentheses on the title line to indicate where to find the current day in the Proper of Saints.

📖 As an example from the Birth of Mary, September 8, from Volume IV, the antiphons are found in the Proper of Saints, and the psalms come from Sunday, Week I.

The reading, responsory, and antiphon for the Canticle of Zechariah are given in the Proper of Saints.

ⓘ The sign of the cross is made at the beginning of the Canticle of Zechariah, and the canticle concludes with *Glory to the Father.*

The intercessions, if not given in the Proper of Saints, are taken from the Commons.

The prayer is given in the Proper of Saints.

📖 As an example from the Birth of Mary, September 8, from Volume IV, the reading and responsory, as well as the antiphon for the Canticle of Zechariah, are all found in the Proper of Saints; the intercessions are found in the Common of the Blessed Virgin Mary; and the prayer is found in the Proper of Saints.

In the absence of a priest or deacon to give a blessing and the dismissal, or in individual recitation, the conclusion (as found in the Ordinary) is as follows:

May the Lord bless us, protect us from all evil, and bring us to everlasting life.
—Amen.

## 24 DAYTIME PRAYER ON FEASTS

(i) Religious who practice the contemplative life may be required to recite all three Hours of Daytime Prayer in choir, but in private recitation "it is permitted to choose from the three Hours the one most appropriate to the time of day" (GILH 77). If it is desired to recite all three Hours, a section of Complimentary Psalmody can be found in each volume between Night Prayer and the Proper of Saints.

Daytime Prayer begins as follows, making *the sign of the cross* (from forehead to breast and from left shoulder to right shoulder) at the words, "God, come to my assistance," and *bowing the head* during the words, "Glory to the Father, and to the Son, and to the Holy Spirit":

God, come to my assistance.
—Lord, make haste to help me.
Glory to the Father, and to the Son, and to the
    Holy Spirit:

as it was in the beginning, is now, and will be
forever. Amen. (Alleluia.)

ⓘ For musical purposes, the invocation "God" may
be expanded, for example, "O God," etc., as per
the Ordinary.

☑ *Alleluia* is omitted during Lent.

The hymn is found in the Ordinary, unless given in the
Proper of Saints.

The antiphons may come from the current weekday, the
Proper of Seasons, the Proper of Saints, or the Commons, *as directed in the Proper of Saints.*

When only one daytime hour is said, the psalms are
taken from the current weekday, unless given in the
Proper of Saints.

If the reading and verse are not given in the Proper of
Saints, the Proper will direct you to the appropriate
Commons.

The prayer is given in the Proper of Saints.

📖 As an example from The Birth of Mary, note that
September 8 could occur on any day of the week;
therefore, the antiphons are given in the Proper

of Saints and the psalms come from the appropriate week and day of the Psalter; the readings and their responsories come from the Proper of Saints; and the Prayer is as in Morning Prayer.

The conclusion (as found in the Ordinary) is as follows:

Let us praise the Lord.
—And give Him thanks.

## 25  EVENING PRAYER ON FEASTS

☑ If a solemnity follows the current day, then Evening Prayer I of the solemnity is usually celebrated, not the Evening Prayer II of the current feast. Remember, Sundays are always celebrated as solemnities, so Evening Prayer on Saturday feasts is usually Evening Prayer I of the following Sunday.

Evening Prayer begins as follows, making *the sign of the cross* (from forehead to breast and from left shoulder to right shoulder) at the words, "God, come to my assistance," and *bowing the head* during the words, "Glory to the Father, and to the Son, and to the Holy Spirit":

God, come to my assistance.
—Lord, make haste to help me.
Glory to the Father, and to the Son, and to the
    Holy Spirit:
as it was in the beginning, is now, and will be
    forever. Amen. (Alleluia.)

(i) For musical purposes, the invocation "God" may be expanded, for example, "O God," etc., as per the Ordinary.

☑ *Alleluia* is omitted during Lent.

The hymn, if not specified by the Proper of Saints, should be taken from the Commons.

The antiphons, if not given in or specified by the Proper of Saints, are taken, along with the psalms and canticle, from the specified Common.

📖 Notice how SJG gives a number in parentheses on the title line to indicate where to find the current day in the Proper of Saints. Plus, on the next line SJG will say, "From Com of" with the name of the Common and the page number.

📖 As an example from the Birth of Mary, September 8, from Volume IV, the antiphons are found in the Proper of Saints, and the psalms are from the Common of the Blessed Virgin Mary.

The reading, responsory, and antiphon for the Canticle of Mary, if not given in the Proper of Saints, are taken from the specified Commons.

(i) The sign of the cross is made at the beginning of

the Canticle of Mary, and the canticle concludes
with *Glory to the Father.*

The intercessions, if not given in the Proper of Saints,
are taken from the Commons.

The prayer is given in the Proper of Saints.

📖 As an example from the Birth of Mary, September
8, from Volume IV, the reading and the responsory, as well as the antiphon for the Canticle of
Mary, are all found in the Proper of Saints; the intercessions are from the Common of the Blessed
Virgin Mary; and the prayer is found in the Proper
of Saints.

In the absence of a priest or deacon to give a blessing
and the dismissal, or in individual recitation, the conclusion (as found in the Ordinary) is as follows:

May the Lord bless us, protect us from all evil, and
bring us to everlasting life.
—Amen.

## 26  NIGHT PRAYER ON FEASTS

---

You may find it helpful to have a permanent ribbon marking the beginning of this section because Night Prayer always begins at the same place.

Night Prayer begins as follows, making *the sign of the cross* (from forehead to breast and from left shoulder to right shoulder) at the words, "God, come to my assistance," and *bowing the head* during the words, "Glory to the Father, and to the Son, and to the Holy Spirit":

> God, come to my assistance.
> —Lord, make haste to help me.
> Glory to the Father, and to the Son, and to the
>     Holy Spirit:
> as it was in the beginning, is now, and will be
>     forever. Amen. (Alleluia.)

ⓘ For musical purposes, the invocation "God" may
   be expanded; for example, "O God," etc., as per

the Ordinary.

☑ *Alleluia* is omitted during Lent.

Then a brief examination of conscience may be made as you review the events of the day.

Everything is found in the Night Prayer section, according to the day of the week.

ⓘ If the following day is a solemnity, use the section of Night Prayer called "After Evening Prayer I on Sundays and Solemnities".

📖 SJG will say, "NP" plus a number, to direct you to the appropriate page of the Night Prayer.

☑ During *Lent*, the alleluias at the end of each verse of the responsory are not said.

During the *Easter Triduum*, in place of the responsory, the antiphon "For our sake Christ was obedient, accepting even death [etc. as per the day]" is said.

During the *Octave of Easter*, in place of the responsory, the following antiphon is said: "This is the day the Lord has made; let us rejoice and be glad, alleluia."

(i) The sign of the cross is made at the beginning of the Gospel canticle, and the canticle concludes with *Glory to the Father.*

The conclusion for Night Prayer is as follows:

May the all-powerful Lord grant us a restful
  night and a peaceful death.
—Amen.

Then one of the antiphons in honor of the Blessed Virgin Mary is said; these antiphons are found at the very end of the Night Prayer section.

- The *Alma Redemptoris Mater* (Loving Mother of the Redeemer) is traditionally recited from the First Sunday of Advent to the Feast of the Presentation.

- The *Ave Regina Cœlorum* (Hail, Queen of the Heavens) is traditionally recited from after the Presentation to Holy Saturday.

- The *Regina Cœli* (Queen of Heaven) is traditionally recited from Easter Sunday to Pentecost Sunday.

- The *Salve Regina* (Hail, Holy Queen) is traditionally recited from after Pentecost until the First Sunday of Advent.

# 27 GRAPHIC SUMMARY: FEASTS

*Feasts*

| Proper of Seasons | Ordinary | Psalter | Proper of Saints | Commons |
|---|---|---|---|---|
|  |  |  | Antiphon. |  |
|  | Psalm. |  |  |  |

## OFFICE OF READINGS

*Feasts*

| Proper of Seasons | Ordinary | Psalter | Proper of Saints | Commons |
|---|---|---|---|---|
|  |  |  | Hymn; psalmody, antiphons, and verse; first reading and responsory.<br><br>(If not given in the Proper of Saints, directions will be given to use the Commons.) |  |
|  |  |  | Second reading and responsory. |  |
|  | Hymn *Te Deum*. |  |  |  |
|  |  |  | Prayer. |  |

# Morning Prayer
## *Feasts*

| Proper of Seasons | Ordinary | Psalter | Proper of Saints | Commons |
|---|---|---|---|---|
| | | Hymn.<br><br>(Use the Commons or the weekday if not given in the Proper of Saints.) | | |
| | | | Antiphons.<br><br>(If not given in or specified by the Proper of Saints, use the Commons.) | |
| | | Psalmody (from Sunday, Week I). | | |
| | | | Reading, responsory, antiphon for the Canticle of Zechariah, intercessions, and prayer.<br><br>(If not given in or specified by the Proper of Saints, use the Commons.) | |

## Daytime Prayer

*Feasts*

| Ordinary | Proper of Seasons | Psalter | Proper of Saints | Commons |
|---|---|---|---|---|
| Hymn, unless given in the Proper of Seasons. | | | | |
| | Antiphons (as directed in the Proper of Saints). | | | |
| | | Psalmody, unless given in the Proper of Saints. | | |
| | | | Reading and verse. (If not given in the Proper of Saints, use the Commons.) | |
| | | | Prayer. | |

# Evening Prayer

*Feasts*

| Proper of Seasons | Ordinary | Psalter | Proper of Saints | Commons |
|---|---|---|---|---|
| | | | Hymn.<br><br>(Use the Commons if not given in the Proper of Saints.) | |
| | | | Antiphons.<br><br>(If not given in or specified by the Proper of Saints, use the Commons.) | |
| | | | | Psalmody. |
| | | | Reading, responsory, antiphon for the Canticle of Mary, intercessions, and prayer.<br><br>(If not given in or specified by the Proper of Saints, use the Commons.) | |

## 28   SOLEMNITIES

All Sundays are celebrated as solemnities. In addition, other fixed dates of the year, such as Mary, Mother of God (January 1), Joseph, Husband of Mary (March 19), the Annunciation (March 25), the Birth of John the Baptist (June 24), Peter and Paul, Apostles (June 29), the Assumption of the Blessed Virgin (August 15), All Saints (November 1), the Immaculate conception (December 8), and Christmas (December 25), are celebrated as solemnities. (The dates of other solemnities of the year are movable and ultimately depend on the date of Easter). All weekdays within the Octave of Christmas and the Octave of Easter are also celebrated as solemnities.

On Sundays in Ordinary Time, the material comes from both the Psalter and the Proper of Seasons.

On Sundays outside of Ordinary Time more material comes from the Proper of Seasons than during Ordinary Time.

On fixed solemnities, even if they occur on a Sunday, everything comes primarily from one section of the breviary: either the Proper of Saints or the Proper of Seasons.

On some movable solemnities, everything comes from the Proper of Seasons; on other movable solemnities, the material comes from both the Psalter and the Proper of Seasons.

*Remember: At the beginning of each day, check the day in the SJG, and, if the day is a solemnity, place a ribbon in the appropriate sections of the Proper of Seasons, the Psalter, and the Proper of Saints as necessary.*

## 29 THE INVITATORY ON SOLEMNITIES

The invitatory belongs at the beginning of each day of prayer, so you may find it helpful to have a ribbon permanently at its place in the Ordinary.

The invitatory begins as follows:

Lord, open my lips.
—And my mouth will proclaim your praise.

*(Make the sign of the cross on your lips with the side of your thumb as you say these words, per GILH 266.)*

Then Psalm 95 (or, if you prefer, Psalm 100, 67, or 24) and its antiphon follows.

On Sundays in Ordinary Time, the antiphon is taken from the Psalter. On Sundays outside Ordinary Time, the antiphon will be given in the Proper of Seasons. On other solemnities not on a Sunday, the antiphon will be specified in the Proper of Saints or the Proper of Seasons.

📖 The SJG will say "ALL" with a number to direct you to the page of the Psalter or the Proper of Saints or the Proper of Seasons where the Office begins.

After "Lord, open my lips . . ." is said, the antiphon is recited and immediately *repeated*. Then the first strophe of the psalm is said, then the antiphon is said, then the next strophe of the psalm is said, then the antiphon is said, and so on. Then the *Glory to the Father* is said, and then the antiphon is recited again to conclude.

ⓘ As indicated in the Ordinary, in individual recitation the antiphon need not be said after each strophe of the psalm; that is, the antiphon can be said only at the beginning of the psalm and following the *Glory to the Father*.

## 30 THE OFFICE OF READINGS ON SOLEMNITIES

---

ⓘ The Office of Readings "may be recited at any hour of the day" (GILH 59); many persons, especially in individual recitation, prefer to celebrate the Office of Readings in the morning, immediately before Morning Prayer. That preference will be followed in this present book.

*Sundays in Ordinary Time*

On Sundays in Ordinary Time, the hymn is taken from the Psalter.

📖 SJG will say "ALL" with a number to indicate the page of the Psalter where the Office of the day begins. You will find the hymn itself in the section for the Office of Readings.

ⓘ When the Office of Readings comes immediately before Morning Prayer, the hymn designated for the latter may be used in place of the hymn at the beginning of the Office of Readings.

**The psalmody, antiphons, and verse are taken from the Psalter.**

📖 On Sundays in Ordinary Time (with the exception of the *Holy Trinity* and the *Body and Blood of Christ*), SJG will say "ALL" to refer you to the page of the Psalter where the day's Office begins. (For the exceptions mentioned above, the "ALL" refers to the page of the Proper of Seasons where the day's Office begins.)

**The first reading and responsory as well as the second reading and responsory are found in the Proper of Seasons; the Psalter will cue you with the rubric, "Readings and prayer, as in the Office of the day."**

📖 SJG will indicate the location of the readings, etc. with the direction "Rd, Te Deum, Ant & Pr," followed by the page number where the day's Office begins in the Proper of Seasons.

**The hymn *Te Deum* (found in the Ordinary) is said after the responsory for the second reading.**

📖 Notice how SJG says "Te Deum" to remind you of this.

The prayer is given in the Proper of Seasons.

(i) When Morning Prayer follows immediately, the prayer and acclamation at the end of the Office of Readings are not used.

## *Sundays outside Ordinary Time*

On Sundays outside Ordinary Time, the hymn is specified in the Proper of Seasons.

📖 Except for Sundays in Advent (when SJG says "Hymn" plus a number), SJG will say "ALL" with a number to indicate the page of the Proper of Seasons, Psalter, or Proper of Saints where the Office of the day begins. If you don't find the hymn itself in the section for the Office of Readings, or a reference to a page number there, then use a hymn from the appropriate Hymns section (Lenten Season: Before Holy Week; Lenten Season: Holy Week; or Easter Season) in the Proper of Seasons.

(i) When the Office of Readings comes immediately before Morning Prayer, the hymn designated for the latter may be used in place of the hymn at the beginning of the Office of Readings.

The psalmody, antiphons, and verse are taken variously

from the Psalter and the Proper of Seasons.

📖 On Sundays in Lent and Easter (with the exception of Easter Sunday itself, the *Ascension of the Lord*—when it is transferred to a Sunday—and *Pentecost*) SJG will say "ALL" with a number, and "Ps" with a number. The "ALL" refers to the first page of the section in the Proper of Seasons where everything except the psalmody is found; the "Ps" refers to the Psalter where the psalmody is found. In this case you begin with the Psalter and then go to the Proper of Seasons for the verse and the remainder of the Office. (For those exceptions mentioned above, everything comes from the Proper of Seasons, and so SJG simply says "ALL" followed by a number to indicate the page of the Proper of Seasons where the Office begins.)

📖 On Sundays in Advent, SJG will say "OOR" plus a number, "Hymn" plus a number, and "Ps" plus a number to refer you to these various parts. In this case you begin with the Psalter and then go to the Proper of Seasons for the verse and the remainder of the Office.

The first reading and responsory, and the second reading and responsory are found in the Proper of Seasons; when the psalmody comes from the Psalter, after the last psalm there will be a rubric that says, "Verse, readings and prayer, as in the Office of the day," to remind you to then turn to the Proper of Seasons.

📖 On Sundays in Lent and Easter, the number following the "ALL" in the SJG will take you to the page where the day's Office begins in the Proper of Seasons.

📖 On Sundays during Advent, the number following the "OOR" in the SJG will take you to the page where the day's Office begins in the Proper of Seasons.

The hymn *Te Deum* (found in the Ordinary) is said after the responsory for the second reading.

📖 Notice how SJG says "Te Deum" to remind you of this.

The prayer is given in the Proper of Seasons.

ⓘ When Morning Prayer follows immediately, the prayer and acclamation at the end of the Office of Readings are not used.

### *Solemnities not on a Sunday*

On other solemnities not on a Sunday, the hymn will

be specified in the Proper of Saints or in the Proper of Seasons.

📖 SJG will say "ALL" with a number to indicate the page of the Proper of Saints (or the Proper of Seasons) where the Office of the day begins. If you don't find the hymn itself in the section for the Office of Readings, you will be told where to take the hymn.

ⓘ When the Office of Readings comes immediately before Morning Prayer, the hymn designated for the latter may be used in place of the hymn at the beginning of the Office of Readings.

The psalmody, antiphons, and verse will be specified in the Proper of Saints (or in the Proper of Seasons, as with the *Ascension of the Lord*).

📖 SJG will say "ALL" to refer you to the page of the Proper of Saints (or the Proper of Seasons) where everything begins.

Both the first reading and the second reading will be given in the Proper of Saints.

☑ Exceptions to this are the *Ascension of the Lord* and the *Sacred Heart*, both non-Sunday solemnities whose Office comes entirely from the Proper of Seasons.

📖 On other solemnities not on a Sunday, the number following the "ALL" in the SJG will take you to the page where the day's Office begins in the Proper of Saints (or Proper of Seasons).

The hymn *Te Deum* (found in the Ordinary) is said after the responsory for the second reading.

📖 Notice how SJG says "Te Deum" to remind you of this.

The prayer will be given in the day's Proper (Saints or Seasons).

ⓘ When Morning Prayer follows immediately, the prayer and acclamation at the end of the Office of Readings are not used.

# 31 MORNING PRAYER ON SOLEMNITIES

Morning Prayer begins as follows, making *the sign of the cross* (from forehead to breast and from left shoulder to right shoulder) at the words, "God, come to my assistance," and *bowing the head* during the words, "Glory to the Father, and to the Son, and to the Holy Spirit":

God, come to my assistance.
—Lord, make haste to help me.
Glory to the Father, and to the Son, and to the
    Holy Spirit:
as it was in the beginning, is now, and will be
    forever. Amen. (Alleluia.)

ⓘ When Morning Prayer follows immediately after the Office of Readings, the introductory *God, come to my assistance* and the *Glory to the Father* are omitted, as per the Ordinary.

ⓘ For musical purposes, the invocation "God" may

be expanded, for example, "O God," etc., as per the Ordinary.

☑ *Alleluia* is omitted during Lent.

### Sundays in Ordinary Time

On Sundays in Ordinary Time, everything is taken from the Psalter, except the antiphon for the Canticle of Zechariah and the prayer, which are given in the Proper of Seasons.

☑ Three exceptions to the above are *Trinity Sunday, Corpus Christi* (when it is celebrated on a Sunday), and *Christ the King*; on these days, everything is taken from the Proper of Seasons except for the psalms and canticle, which are taken from Sunday, Week I of the Psalter.

📖 Notice how SJG says "ALL" plus a number referring to the page of the Psalter where the day's Office begins, and "Rd, Te Deum, Ant & Pr" plus a number referring to the page in the Proper of Seasons where the day's Office begins. After locating the sections in the Psalter and in the Proper of Seasons for Morning Prayer, you begin in the Psalter with the antiphons and psalmody, then go to the Proper of Seasons for the antiphon for the

Canticle of Zechariah, and, after the canticle, go back to the Psalter for the intercessions, and then go back to the Proper of Seasons for the closing prayer, which is always proper to the day.

(i) The sign of the cross is made at the beginning of the Canticle of Zechariah, and the canticle concludes with *Glory to the Father.*

## Sundays outside Ordinary Time

On Sundays outside Ordinary Time, if everything isn't found in the Proper of Seasons, instructions there will tell you where to find the material.

(i) If you don't find the hymn itself in the section for Morning Prayer in the Proper of Seasons, or if you don't find a reference to a page number there, then use a hymn from the Hymns section for the appropriate liturgical season.

(📖) For Sundays in Lent and Easter, SJG may say "ALL" plus a number referring to the page of the Proper of Seasons where the day's Office begins, and "Ps" plus a number referring to the page in the Psalter where the day's Office begins. After locating the sections in the Psalter and the Proper of Seasons for Morning Prayer, you begin with the Psalter for the antiphons and psalmody, then go to the Proper of Seasons for the remainder of the Office. (Notice that the antiphons are given in both the Proper of Seasons and in the Psalter.)

📖 On Sundays during Advent, SJG will say "MP" plus a number, "Hymn" plus a number, and "Ps" plus a number to refer you to these various parts.

ⓘ The sign of the cross is made at the beginning of the Canticle of Zechariah, and the canticle concludes with *Glory to the Father*.

### *Solemnities not on a Sunday*

On all solemnities not on a Sunday, everything will be specified in the Proper of Saints or in the Proper of Seasons.

☑ For all of these solemnities, the psalms and canticle come from Sunday, Week I in the Psalter; the Proper will specify this.

📖 SJG will say "ALL" to refer you to the page of the Proper of Saints (or, in some cases, the Proper of Seasons) where the day's Office begins.

ⓘ The sign of the cross is made at the beginning of

the Canticle of Zechariah, and the canticle concludes with *Glory to the Father.*

The conclusion of the Hour is the same whether during
Ordinary Time or outside Ordinary Time. In the absence of a priest or deacon to give a blessing and the
dismissal, or in individual recitation, the conclusion (as
found in the Ordinary) is as follows:

May the Lord bless us, protect us from all evil and
bring us to everlasting life.
—Amen.

# 32 DAYTIME PRAYER ON SOLEMNITIES

---

(i) Religious who practice the contemplative life may be required to recite all three Hours of Daytime Prayer in choir, but in private recitation "it is permitted to choose from the three Hours the one most appropriate to the time of day" (GILH 77). If it is desired to recite all three Hours, a section of Complimentary Psalmody can be found in each volume between Night Prayer and the Proper of Saints.

Daytime Prayer begins as follows, making *the sign of the cross* (from forehead to breast and from left shoulder to right shoulder) at the words, "God, come to my assistance," and *bowing the head* during the words, "Glory to the Father, and to the Son, and to the Holy Spirit":

God, come to my assistance.
—Lord, make haste to help me.
Glory to the Father, and to the Son, and to the
    Holy Spirit:

as it was in the beginning, is now, and will be
forever. Amen. (Alleluia.)

ⓘ For musical purposes, the invocation "God" may
be expanded, for example, "O God," etc., as per
the Ordinary.

☑ *Alleluia* is omitted during Lent.

## Sundays in Ordinary Time

On Sundays in Ordinary Time, the hymn is found in
the Ordinary; everything else is found in the Psalter,
except the prayer, which comes from the Proper of
Seasons. Note that for (a) *Trinity Sunday,* (b) *Corpus
Christi [the Body and Blood of Christ]* when it is celebrated on a Sunday, and (c) *Christ the King,* the antiphons and readings are given in the Proper of Seasons.

📖 For Sundays in Ordinary Time, SJG says "ALL" plus
a number to direct you to the Psalter, and "Rd,
Te Deum, Ant & Pr" plus a number to direct you
to the Proper of Seasons; understand that those
numbers take you to the *beginning* of the Office
of the day in those particular sections. You must
then turn to the appropriate pages for the Daytime Prayer, beginning with the Psalter for all of
the Office except the prayer, then going to the

Proper of Seasons for the prayer.

### *Sundays outside Ordinary Time*

On Easter Sunday, the Sunday within the Octave of Easter, and *Pentecost*, everything is given in the Proper of Seasons. On all other Sundays outside Ordinary Time the hymn and antiphons are specified in the Proper of Seasons; the psalmody is found in the Psalter according to the liturgical week of that Sunday; and the reading, verse, and prayer are found in the Proper of Seasons.

☑ On those Sundays when the psalms come from the Psalter, a rubric in the Psalter will cue you to turn to the Proper of Seasons for the remainder of the Office by saying, "Reading, verse and prayer, as in the Office of the day."

📖 When SJG says "ALL" plus a number to direct you to the Proper of Seasons, and "Ps" plus a number to direct you to the Psalter, understand that those numbers take you to the *beginning* of the Office of the day in those particular sections. You must then turn to the appropriate pages for the Day-time Prayer.

📖 On days when SJG says "DP" followed by a number, that will take you to the page of the Psalter where Daytime Prayer begins.

### *Solemnities not on Sundays*

For solemnities not occurring on Sundays, instructions will be given in the Proper of Saints or in the Proper of Seasons.

☑ Some solemnities (such as the *Assumption of the Blessed Virgin*) specify the use of the Complementary Psalms (also called Gradual Psalms). These psalms are found at the very end of the Psalter, right after the Night Prayer section. Just follow the instructions in the Proper of Saints.

📖 SJG will say "DP Ps" plus a number to refer you to the appropriate location of the psalmody.

The conclusion (as found in the Ordinary) is as follows:

Let us praise the Lord.
—And give Him thanks.

## 33  EVENING PRAYER
   ON SOLEMNITIES

☑  If another solemnity follows the current day, (such as when the *Immaculate Conception of Mary* occurs on a Saturday and is followed by the Second Sunday of Advent), then Evening Prayer I of the following solemnity is usually celebrated, not the Evening Prayer II of the current day. One exception to this general rule is when Christmas occurs on a Saturday; in this case, Evening Prayer II of Christmas takes precedence over Evening Prayer I of the following Sunday.

Evening Prayer begins as follows, making *the sign of the cross* (from forehead to breast and from left shoulder to right shoulder) at the words, "God, come to my assistance," and *bowing the head* during the words, "Glory to the Father, and to the Son, and to the Holy Spirit":

God, come to my assistance.
—Lord, make haste to help me.
Glory to the Father, and to the Son, and to the

Holy Spirit:
as it was in the beginning, is now, and will be
   forever. Amen. (Alleluia.)

ⓘ  For musical purposes, the invocation "God" may
   be expanded, for example, "O God," etc., as per
   the Ordinary.

☑  *Alleluia* is omitted during Lent.

*Sundays in Ordinary Time*

On Sundays in Ordinary Time, everything is taken
from the Psalter, except the antiphon for the Canticle
of Mary and the prayer, which are given in the Proper
of Seasons.

☑  Three exceptions to the above are *Trinity Sunday,
   Corpus Christi* (when it is celebrated on a Sunday),
   and *Christ the King*; on these days, everything is
   taken from the Proper of Seasons.

📖  Notice how SJG says "ALL" plus a number referring
   to the page of the Psalter where the day's Office
   begins, and "Rd, Te Deum, Ant & Pr" plus a number referring to the page in the Proper of Seasons
   where the day's Office begins. After locating the
   sections in the Psalter and in the Proper of Sea-

sons for Evening Prayer, you begin in the Psalter with the antiphons and psalmody, then go to the Proper of Seasons for the antiphon for the Canticle of Mary, and, after the canticle, go back to the Psalter for the intercessions, and then go back to the Proper of Seasons for the closing prayer, which is always proper to the day.

ⓘ The sign of the cross is made at the beginning of the Canticle of Mary, and the canticle concludes with *Glory to the Father*.

### *Sundays outside Ordinary Time*

On Sundays outside Ordinary Time, if everything isn't found in the Proper of Seasons, instructions there will tell you where to find the material.

ⓘ If you don't find the hymn itself in the section for Evening Prayer in the Proper of Seasons, or a reference to a page number there, then use a hymn from the appropriate Hymns section for the liturgical season.

📖 For Sundays in Lent and Easter, SJG may say "ALL" plus a number referring to the page of the Proper of Seasons where the day's Office begins, and "Ps" plus a number referring to the page in the Psalter where the day's Office begins. After locating the sections in the Psalter and the Proper of Seasons for Evening Prayer, you begin with the Psalter for the antiphons and psalmody, then go to the Proper of Seasons for the remainder of the Office. (Notice that the antiphons are given in both the Proper of Seasons and in the Psalter.)

📖 On Sundays during Advent, SJG will say "EPI (of Sunday)" on the previous Saturday, if it is a Memorial or Feast, to remind you to celebrate Evening Prayer I of Sunday rather than Evening Prayer II of the Memorial or Feast, and then, for the Sunday itself, SJG will say "EPII" plus a number, "Hymn" plus a number, and "Ps" plus a number, to refer you to these various parts on Sunday.

ⓘ The sign of the cross is made at the beginning of the Canticle of Mary, and the canticle concludes with *Glory to the Father.*

### *Solemnities not on a Sunday*

On all solemnities not on a Sunday, everything will be specified in the Proper of Saints or the Proper of Seasons.

☑ For those solemnities found in the Proper of Saints, the psalms and canticle come from the appropriate Commons; the Proper will specify this, and it will also provide the antiphons.

☑ For those solemnities that are found in the Proper of Seasons (such as the *Sacred Heart* or *Corpus Christi* when it is not celebrated on a Sunday), the psalms and canticle will also be provided by the Proper of Seasons.

📖 SJG will say "ALL" to refer you to the page of the Proper of Saints (or, in some cases, the Proper of Seasons) where the day's Office begins.

ⓘ The sign of the cross is made at the beginning of the Canticle of Mary, and the canticle concludes with *Glory to the Father*.

The conclusion of the Hour is the same whether during Ordinary Time or outside Ordinary Time. In the absence of a priest or deacon to give a blessing and the dismissal, or in individual recitation, the conclusion (as found in the Ordinary) is as follows:

May the Lord bless us, protect us from all evil and bring us to everlasting life.
—Amen.

## 34 NIGHT PRAYER ON SOLEMNITIES

You may find it helpful to have a permanent ribbon marking the beginning of this section because Night Prayer always begins at the same place.

Night Prayer begins as follows, making *the sign of the cross* (from forehead to breast and from left shoulder to right shoulder) at the words, "God, come to my assistance," and *bowing the head* during the words, "Glory to the Father, and to the Son, and to the Holy Spirit":

God, come to my assistance.
—Lord, make haste to help me.
Glory to the Father, and to the Son, and to the
    Holy Spirit:
as it was in the beginning, is now, and will be
    forever. Amen. (Alleluia.)

ⓘ For musical purposes, the invocation "God" may
be expanded; for example, "O God," etc., as per

the Ordinary.

☑    *Alleluia* is omitted during Lent.

Then a brief examination of conscience may be made as you review the events of the day.

Everything is found in the Night Prayer section, according to the day of the week.

ⓘ   On the night before the Solemnity, use the section of Night Prayer called "After Evening Prayer I on Sundays and Solemnities." On the night of the Solemnity itself, use the section of Night Prayer called "After Evening Prayer II on Sundays and Solemnities," but if the next day is also a solemnity, you may use either Evening Prayer I or Evening Prayer II.

📖   SJG will say, "NP" plus a number, to direct you to the appropriate page of the Night Prayer.

☑   During *Lent*, the alleluias at the end of each verse of the responsory are not said.

During the *Easter Triduum*, in place of the responsory, the antiphon "For our sake Christ was obedient, accepting even death [etc. as per the day]" is said.

During the *Octave of Easter*, in place of the responsory, the following antiphon is said: "This is the day the Lord has made; let us rejoice and be glad, alleluia."

ⓘ The sign of the cross is made at the beginning of the Gospel canticle, and the canticle concludes with *Glory to the Father.*

The conclusion for Night Prayer is as follows:

May the all-powerful Lord grant us a restful
     night and a peaceful death.
—Amen.

Then one of the antiphons in honor of the Blessed Virgin Mary is said; these antiphons are found at the very end of the Night Prayer section.

- The *Alma Redemptoris Mater* (Loving Mother of the Redeemer) is traditionally recited from the First Sunday of Advent to the Feast of the Presentation.

- The *Ave Regina Cælorum* (Hail, Queen of the Heavens) is traditionally recited from after the Presentation to Holy Saturday.

- The *Regina Cæli* (Queen of Heaven) is traditionally

recited from Easter Sunday to Pentecost Sunday.

- The *Salve Regina* (Hail, Holy Queen) is traditionally recited from after Pentecost until the First Sunday of Advent.

# 35  GRAPHIC SUMMARY: SOLEMNITIES

## Invitatory
### Sundays

| Proper of Seasons | Ordinary | Psalter | Proper of Saints | Commons |
|---|---|---|---|---|
|  |  |  | Antiphon. |  |
|  | Psalm. |  |  |  |

## Invitatory
### Sundays Outside Ordinary Time

| Proper of Seasons | Ordinary | Psalter | Proper of Saints | Commons |
|---|---|---|---|---|
| Antiphon. |  |  |  |  |
|  | Psalm. |  |  |  |

## Invitatory
### Solemnities not on a Sunday

| Proper of Seasons | Ordinary | Psalter | Proper of Saints | Commons |
|---|---|---|---|---|
| Antiphon (unless given in the Proper of Saints). | | | Antiphon (unless given in the Proper of Seasons). | |
| | Psalm. | | | |

## Office of Readings
### Sundays

| Proper of Seasons | Ordinary | Psalter | Proper of Saints | Commons |
|---|---|---|---|---|
| | | Hymn, psalmody, antiphons, and verse. | | |
| First reading and responsory and second reading and responsory. | | | | |
| | Hymn *Te Deum*. | | | |
| Prayer. | | | | |

## Office of Readings
### *Sundays Outside Ordinary Time*

| Ordinary | Proper of Seasons | Psalter | Proper of Saints | Commons |
|---|---|---|---|---|
|  | Hymn. |  |  |  |
|  | Psalmody, antiphons, and verse (as directed). |  |  |  |
|  | First reading and responsory and second reading and responsory. |  |  |  |
| Hymn *Te Deum*. |  |  |  |  |
|  | Prayer. |  |  |  |

## OFFICE OF READINGS
*Solemnities not on a Sunday*

| Ordinary | Psalter | Proper of Seasons | Proper of Saints | Commons |
|---|---|---|---|---|
| | | Hymn. | | |
| | | Psalmody, antiphons, and verse. | | |
| | | First reading and responsory and second reading and responsory. | | |
| Hymn *Te Deum*. | | | | |
| | | Prayer. | | |

## Morning Prayer
### *Sundays*
(Except for *Trinity Sunday* and *The Body and Blood of Christ*)

| Proper of Seasons | Ordinary | Psalter | Proper of Saints | Commons |
|---|---|---|---|---|
| | | Hymn, antiphons, psalmody, reading, and responsory. | | |
| Antiphon for the Canticle of Zechariah. | | | | |
| | | Intercessions. | | |
| Prayer. | | | | |

## Morning Prayer
*Sundays Outside Ordinary Time*

(Except for *Easter Sunday*, the Sunday within the Octave of Easter, and *Pentecost*)

| Proper of Seasons | Ordinary | Psalter | Proper of Saints | Commons |
|---|---|---|---|---|
| Hymn. | | | | |
| | | Antiphons and psalmody. | | |
| Reading, responsory, antiphon for the Canticle of Zechariah, intercessions, and prayer. | | | | |

## Morning Prayer
*Solemnities not on a Sunday*

| Ordinary | Psalter | Proper of Seasons | Proper of Saints | Commons |
|---|---|---|---|---|
| | | Hymn and antiphons. | | |
| | Psalmody. | | | |
| | | Reading, responsory, antiphon for the Canticle of Zechariah, intercessions, and prayer. | | |

## DAYTIME PRAYER
### *Sundays*

(Except for *Trinity Sunday* and *The Body and Blood of Christ*)

| Ordinary | Proper of Seasons | Psalter | Proper of Saints | Commons |
|----------|-------------------|---------|------------------|---------|
| Hymn. | | | | |
| | | Antiphons, psalmody, reading, and verse. | | |
| | Prayer. | | | |

## DAYTIME PRAYER
### *Sundays Outside Ordinary Time*

(Except for *Easter Sunday*, the Sunday within the Octave of Easter, and *Pentecost*)

| Ordinary | Proper of Seasons | Psalter | Proper of Saints | Commons |
|----------|-------------------|---------|------------------|---------|
| | Hymn and antiphons. | | | |
| | | Psalmody. | | |
| | Reading, verse, and prayer. | | | |

## Daytime Prayer

### Solemnities not on a Sunday

| Ordinary | Psalter | Proper of Seasons | Proper of Saints | Commons |
|---|---|---|---|---|
| | | (Follow instructions in Proper of Seasons or Proper of Saints.) | | |

## Evening Prayer

### Sundays

(Except for *Trinity Sunday* and *The Body and Blood of Christ*)

| Proper of Seasons | Ordinary | Psalter | Proper of Saints | Commons |
|---|---|---|---|---|
| | | Hymn, antiphons, psalmody, reading, and responsory. | | |
| Antiphon for the Canticle of Mary. | | | | |
| | | Intercessions. | | |
| Prayer. | | | | |

## Evening Prayer
### *Sundays Outside Ordinary Time*

(Except for *Easter Sunday*, the Sunday within the Octave of Easter, and *Pentecost*)

| Proper of Seasons | Ordinary | Psalter | Proper of Saints | Commons |
|---|---|---|---|---|
| Hymn. | | | | |
| | | Antiphons and psalmody. | | |
| Reading, responsory, antiphon for the Canticle of Mary, intercessions, and prayer. | | | | |

## Evening Prayer
*Solemnities not on a Sunday*

| Ordinary | Psalter | Proper of Seasons | Proper of Saints | Commons |
|---|---|---|---|---|
| | | Hymn and antiphons (as directed). | | |
| | Psalmody. | | | |
| | | Reading, responsory, antiphon for the Canticle of Mary, intercessions, and prayer (as directed). | | |

# APPENDICES

# APPENDIX I:
## "WALK-THROUGH" MEMORIAL

*Memorial*
PRESENTATION OF MARY
November 21

### Invitatory

Begin with "Lord, open my lips., etc." Take the *antiphon* for the Invitatory from the Common of the Blessed Virgin Mary. Notice that two antiphons are offered; you may choose either one according to personal preference. Turn to the Ordinary for the *invitatory psalm*.

### Office of Readings

Take the *hymn* from the Common of the Blessed Virgin Mary—or use the hymn of the current weekday, if you prefer. (If the Morning Prayer will directly follow the Office of Readings, you may use the hymn for Morning Prayer.) Take the *antiphons and psalms* from the Psalter, according to the current weekday. Then turn to the current day in the Proper of Seasons for the *first reading* and its *responsory*. Turn then to the Proper of Saints for the *second reading* and its *responsory*. The *prayer*, given in the Proper of Saints, is not said if Morning Prayer directly follows the Office of Readings.

**Morning Prayer**

Begin with "God, come to my assistance, etc." Take the *hymn* from the Common of the Blessed Virgin Mary—or from the current weekday, if you prefer. (If the Office of Readings immediately preceded Morning Prayer, and you used the hymn for Morning Prayer at that time, then you need not sing or recite any hymn now.) Turn to the current weekday of the Psalter for the *psalms and canticle* and their *antiphons*. Then turn to the Common of the Blessed Virgin Mary for the *reading and responsory*—or you may take them from the current weekday, if you prefer. Find the *antiphon* for the Canticle of Zechariah in the Proper of Saints, turning to the Ordinary for the Canticle of Zechariah itself. Return to the Common of the Blessed Virgin Mary for the *intercessions*—or you may take them from the current weekday, if you prefer. Then say the *Our Father* from memory, followed by the *prayer* given in the Proper of Saints. Conclude with "May the Lord bless us, etc."

**Daytime Prayer**

Everything is taken from the current weekday.

**Evening Prayer**

ⓘ  You will find a section for Evening Prayer I in all of the Commons, but this section is not used on memorials. On a memorial, then, be careful to use the section of the Common called Evening Prayer II.

*The Evening Prayer of a memorial is not said if the next day is a Sunday or a solemnity, in which case Evening Prayer I of the Sunday or solemnity is said.*

Begin with "God, come to my assistance, etc." Take the *hymn* from the Common of the Blessed Virgin Mary— or from the current weekday, if you prefer. Turn to the current weekday of the Psalter for the *psalms and canticle* and their *antiphons*. Then turn to the Common of the Blessed Virgin Mary for the *reading and responsory*—or you may take them from the current weekday, if you prefer. Find the *antiphon* for the Canticle of Mary in the Proper of Saints, turning to the Ordinary for the Canticle of Mary itself. Return to the Common of the Blessed Virgin Mary for the *intercessions*—or you may take them from the current weekday, if you prefer. Then say the *Our Father* from memory, followed by the *prayer* given in the Proper of Saints. Conclude with "May the Lord bless us, etc."

## Night Prayer

Everything is taken from Night Prayer according to the current day of the week.

# APPENDIX II:
## "WALK-THROUGH" FEAST

Saint Matthias, Apostle
May 14

## Invitatory

Begin with "Lord, open my lips., etc." Take the *antiphon* from the Common of Apostles. Turn to the Ordinary for the *invitatory psalm.*

## Office of Readings

Take the *hymn* from the Common of Apostles. (If Morning Prayer will directly follow the Office of Readings, you may use the hymn for Morning Prayer.) The *antiphons and psalms* and the *first reading* and its *responsory* are also from the Common of Apostles. The *second reading* and its *responsory* is given in the Proper of Saints. Then recite the hymn *Te Deum,* which is found in the Ordinary. The *prayer* is given in the Proper of

Saints but is not said if Morning Prayer directly follows the Office of Readings.

## Morning Prayer

Begin with "God, come to my assistance, etc." The *hymn* is given in the Common of Apostles. (If the Office of Readings immediately preceded Morning Prayer, and you used the hymn for Morning Prayer at that time, then you need not sing or recite any hymn now.) The *psalms and canticle* come from Sunday of Week I in the Psalter, but the *antiphons* to be used are in the Common of Apostles; turn back and forth between those sections, from antiphon to psalm to antiphon and so on. Then turn back to the Common of Apostles for the *reading and responsory*. Because the Proper of Saints provides an *antiphon* for the Canticle of Zechariah, use it rather than the antiphon found in the Common of Apostles. Turn to the Ordinary for the Canticle of Zechariah itself. Take the *intercessions* from the Common of Apostles. Then say the *Our Father* from memory, followed by the *prayer* given in the Proper of Saints. Conclude with "May the Lord bless us, etc."

## Daytime Prayer

Begin with "God, come to my assistance, etc." Take the

hymn from the Ordinary, page 658ff. As directed by the Proper of Saints, the *antiphons and psalms* should be taken from the current day of the week, and the *reading* (according to the appropriate hour) should be taken from the Common of Apostles. Turn back to the Proper of Saints for the *prayer*. Conclude with "Let us praise the Lord, etc."

## Evening Prayer

ⓘ You will find a section for Evening Prayer I in all of the Commons, but this section is not used on feasts. On a feast, then, be careful to use the section of the Common called Evening Prayer II.

*Note that if the day following a feast is a Sunday or a solemnity, then Evening Prayer I of the Sunday or solemnity is said, unless the feast is a major feast of Our Lord.*

Begin with "God, come to my assistance, etc." The *hymn* is given in the Common of Apostles. Unlike Morning Prayer, the *psalms and canticle* as well as the *antiphons* are all given in the Common of Apostles. The *reading and responsory* should also be taken from the Common of Apostles. Because the Proper of Saints provides an *antiphon* for the Canticle of Mary, use it rather than the antiphon found in the Common of Apostles. Turn to the Ordinary for the Canticle of Mary itself. Turn back to the Common of Apostles for the *intercessions*. Then say the *Our Father* from memory, followed by the *prayer* given in the Proper of Saints. Conclude with "May the Lord bless us, etc."

## Night Prayer

Everything is taken from Night Prayer according to the current day of the week.

# APPENDIX III:
## "WALK-THROUGH" SOLEMNITY

*Solemnity not on a Sunday*
SAINT JOSEPH
March 19

☑ If March 19 occurs during Holy Week, then the solemnity of Saint Joseph will be transferred to some day before Holy Week or after Easter. Also, if March 19 occurs on a Sunday, then the solemnity of Saint Joseph will be transferred to the following Monday, March 20.

**Evening Prayer I**

*Said on the evening before the actual solemnity.*

Begin with "God, come to my assistance, etc." The *hymn* is given in the Proper of Saints. The Proper of Saints also provides the *antiphons* for the psalms and canticle, but you must turn back and forth to the Common of Holy Men for the *psalms and canticle* themselves. Then return to the Proper of Saints for the *reading and responsory*. Because March 19 could occur during either Lent or the Easter Season, depending on how early or late Easter occurs, be sure to use the appropriate responsory. The *antiphon* for the Canticle of Mary is given in the Proper of Saints, but you must turn to the Ordinary for the Canticle of Mary itself. Turn back to the Proper of Saints for the *intercessions*. Then say the *Our Father* from memory, followed by the *prayer* given in the Proper of Saints. Conclude with "May the Lord bless us, etc."

### Night Prayer

Take everything from Night Prayer, using the section for "Night Prayer following Evening Prayer I."

### Invitatory

Begin with "Lord, open my lips., etc." Take the *antiphon* from the Proper of Saints. Turn to the Ordinary for the *invitatory psalm.*

### Office of Readings

The *hymn* is given in the Proper of Saints. (If Morning

Prayer will directly follow the Office of Readings, you may use the hymn for Morning Prayer.) The Proper of Saints also provides the *antiphons* for the psalms, but you must turn back and forth to the Common of Holy Men for the *psalms* themselves. The *first reading* and its *responsory* as well as the *second reading* and its *responsory* are all from the Proper of Saints. Remember to recite the hymn *Te Deum*, which is found in the Ordinary. Turn back to the Proper of Saints for the *prayer*, but it is not said if Morning Prayer directly follows the Office of Readings.

**Morning Prayer**

Begin with "God, come to my assistance, etc." The *hymn* is given in the Proper of Saints. The Proper of Saints also provides the *antiphons* for the psalms and canticle, but you must turn back and forth to Sunday, Week I of the Psalter for the *psalms and canticle* themselves. Then return to the Proper of Saints for the *reading and responsory*. Because March 19 could occur during either Lent or the Easter Season, depending on how early or late Easter occurs, be sure to use the appropriate responsory. The *antiphon* for the Canticle of Zechariah is given in the Proper of Saints, but you must turn to the Ordinary for the Canticle of Zechariah itself. Turn back to the Proper of Saints for the *intercessions*. Then say the *Our Father* from memory, followed by the *prayer* given in the Proper of Saints. Conclude with "May the Lord bless us, etc."

## Daytime Prayer

Begin with "God, come to my assistance, etc." Take the hymn from the Ordinary, page 658ff. The *antiphon* and the *reading* (according to the appropriate hour) are given in the Proper of Saints, but you must turn to the complimentary psalmody (in a section immediately following Night Prayer) for the *psalms*. (In cases such as this when only one antiphon is given, it serves for all three psalms; therefore, recite the antiphon, then say each psalm, each followed by the *Glory to the Father*, and then conclude by reciting the antiphon again.) Turn back to the Proper of Saints for the *prayer*. Conclude with "Let us praise the Lord, etc."

## Evening Prayer II

☑ If the next day is a Sunday, then say Evening Prayer I of that Sunday instead of Evening Prayer II of Saint Joseph.

Begin with "God, come to my assistance, etc." The *hymn* is given in the Proper of Saints under Evening Prayer I. The Proper of Saints also provides the *antiphons* for the psalms and canticle, but you must turn to the Common of Holy Men for the *psalms and canticle* themselves. Thus you will turn back and forth from antiphon to psalm and so on. Then return to the Proper of Saints for the *reading and responsory*. Because March 19 could occur during either Lent or the Easter Season, depending on how early or late Easter occurs, be sure to use the appropriate responsory. The *antiphon* for the Canticle of Mary is given in the Proper of Saints, but you must turn to the Ordinary for the Canticle of Mary itself. Turn back to the Proper of Saints for the *intercessions*. Then say the *Our Father* from memory, followed by the *prayer* given in the Proper of Saints. Conclude with "May the Lord bless us, etc."

**Night Prayer**

Take everything from Night Prayer, using the section for "Night Prayer following Evening Prayer II."

# APPENDIX IV: "WALK-THROUGH" SUNDAY IN ADVENT

FOURTH SUNDAY OF ADVENT
*This day has been chosen to illustrate the complexities of Advent between December 17 and December 24.*

ⓘ Each of the days between December 17–24 has its own place in the Proper of Seasons. The Fourth Sunday of Advent, however, has special instructions that apply for each hour of the day. In what follows, you will be alerted to these instructions.

**Evening Prayer I**

*Said on the evening before the actual solemnity.*

Begin with "God, come to my assistance, etc." In the Proper of Seasons, you are told to take the *hymn* from *Hymns For the Advent Season: After December 17, Evening Prayer* which begin on page 133. The Proper of Seasons (page 309) provides the *antiphons* for the psalms and canticle, and it tells you to take the psalms and canticle themselves from the Psalter, Week IV, page 1043. (The *antiphons* for the psalms and canticle are also provided in the Psalter so that you don't have to turn back and forth from the Psalter to the Proper of Seasons.) Then return to the Proper of Seasons for the *reading and responsory.* The *antiphon* for the Canticle of Mary is given in the "Office of the day," which begins on page 322; this day will be the calendar date between December 17 and December 24 on which this Fourth Sunday of Advent falls. Turn to the Ordinary for the Canticle of Mary itself. Turn back to the Proper of Seasons for the *intercessions.* Then say the *Our Father* from memory, followed by the *prayer* given in the Proper of Seasons. Conclude with "May the Lord bless us, etc."

### Night Prayer

Take everything from Night Prayer, using the section for "Night Prayer following Evening Prayer I."

### Invitatory

Begin with "Lord, open my lips., etc." Take the *antiphon* from the Proper of Seasons, unless the calendar date is December 24, in which case take the antiphon from December 24 in the Proper of Seasons, page 376. Turn to the Ordinary for the *invitatory psalm*.

## Office of Readings

The *hymn* comes from page 132, as specified in the Proper of Seasons. (If Morning Prayer will directly follow the Office of Readings, you may use the hymn for Morning Prayer.) The Proper of Seasons (page 311) provides the *antiphons* for the psalms and canticle, and it tells you to take the psalms and canticle themselves from the Psalter, Week IV, page 1048. (The *antiphons* for the psalms and canticle are also provided in the Psalter so that you don't have to turn back and forth from the Psalter to the Proper of Seasons.) The *verse*, *readings*, and *responsories* are all from the "Office of the day" which begins on page 318; choose the appropriate section according to the calendar date of this Sunday. Remember to recite the hymn *Te Deum*, which is found in the Ordinary. Turn back to the Proper of Seasons for the *prayer*, but the prayer is not said if Morning Prayer directly follows the Office of Readings.

## Morning Prayer

☑ If this Sunday occurs on December 24, everything for Morning Prayer is taken from the office of December 24 in the Proper of Seasons, page 381.

Begin with "God, come to my assistance, etc." In the Proper of Seasons, you are told to take the *hymn* from *Hymns For the Advent Season: After December 17, Morning Prayer* which begin on page 132. The Proper of Seasons (page 312) provides the *antiphons* for the psalms and canticle, and it tells you to take the psalms and canticle themselves from the Psalter, Week IV, page 1053. (The *antiphons* for the psalms and canticle are also provided in the Psalter so that you don't have to turn back and forth from the Psalter to the Proper of Seasons.) Then return to the Proper of Seasons for the *reading and responsory.* The *antiphon* for the Canticle of Zechariah is given in the "Office of the day," which begins on page 322; this day will be the calendar date between December 17 and December 23 on which this Fourth Sunday of Advent occurs. (Remember, if this Sunday occurs on December 24, everything for Morning Prayer comes from the office of December 24.) You must turn to the Ordinary for the Canticle of Zechariah itself. Turn back to the Proper of Seasons for the *intercessions.* Then say the *Our Father* from memory, followed by the *prayer* given in the Proper of Seasons. Conclude with "May the Lord bless us, etc."

## Daytime Prayer

☑ If this Sunday occurs on December 24, everything for Daytime Prayer is taken from the office of

December 24 in the Proper of Seasons, page 383.

Begin with "God, come to my assistance, etc." Take the hymn from the Ordinary, page 658; the *antiphon* and the *reading* (according to the appropriate hour) are given in the Proper of Seasons, but turn to the Psalter page 1057 for the *psalms*. (In cases such as this when only one antiphon is given for each hour, the antiphon serves for all three psalms; recite the antiphon, then say each psalm, each followed by the *Glory to the Father*, and then conclude by reciting the antiphon again.) Turn back to the Proper of Seasons for the *prayer*. Conclude with "Let us praise the Lord, etc."


## Evening Prayer II

☑   If this Sunday occurs on December 24, everything for Evening Prayer is taken from Evening Prayer I of Christmas.

Begin with "God, come to my assistance, etc." In the Proper of Seasons, you are told to take the *hymn* from *Hymns For the Advent Season: After December 17, Evening Prayer* beginning on page 133. The Proper of Seasons (page 315) provides the *antiphons* for the psalms and canticle, and it tells you to take the psalms and canticle themselves from the Psalter, Week IV, page 1060. (The *antiphons* for the psalms and canticle are also provided in the Psalter so that you don't have to turn back and forth from the Psalter to the Proper of Seasons.) Then return to the Proper of Seasons for the *reading and responsory*. The *antiphon* for the Canticle of Mary is given in the Office of the day, which begins on page 322; this day will be the calendar date between December 17 and December 23 on which this Fourth Sunday of Advent occurs. (Remember, if this Sunday occurs on December 24, everything for Evening Prayer comes from Evening Prayer I of Christmas.) You must turn to the Ordinary for the Canticle of Mary itself. Turn back to the Proper of Seasons for the *intercessions*. Then say the *Our Father* from memory, followed by the *prayer* given in the Proper of Seasons. Conclude with "May the Lord bless us, etc."

### Night Prayer

Unless the next day is Christmas, take everything from the section for "Night Prayer following Evening Prayer II." If the next day is Christmas, use "Night Prayer following Evening Prayer I."

## APPENDIX V:
## "WALK-THROUGH" WEEKDAY IN
## THE CHRISTMAS SEASON

---

DECEMBER 27
*St. John, Apostle and Evangelist*

☑ If December 27 occurs on a Sunday, then the celebration of St. John is omitted because the solemnity of the Holy Family, on the Sunday within the Octave of Christmas, is celebrated that day.

### Invitatory

Begin with "Lord, open my lips., etc." Take the *antiphon* from the Proper of Saints, page 1261. Turn to the Ordinary for the *invitatory psalm*.

### Office of Readings

Take the *hymn* from the Common of the Apostles, page 1354, as specified in the Proper of Saints. (If Morning Prayer will directly follow the Office of Readings, you may use the hymn for Morning Prayer.) The Proper of Saints provides the *antiphons* for the psalms and canticle, the psalms and canticle themselves, and the *verse, readings,* and *responsories.* Then, after reciting the hymn *Te Deum,* which is found in the Ordinary, turn back to the Proper of Saints for the *prayer;* the prayer is not said if Morning Prayer directly follows the Office of Readings.

**Morning Prayer**

Begin with "God, come to my assistance, etc." As per the Proper of Saints, take the *hymn* from the Common of Apostles. The Proper of Saints provides the *antiphons* for the psalms and canticle, and it tells you to take the psalms and canticle themselves from Sunday, Week I, in the Psalter. Return to the Proper of Saints for the *reading and responsory,* and the *antiphon* for the Canticle of Zechariah. Turn to the Ordinary for the Canticle of Zechariah itself. Turn back to the Proper of Saints for the *intercessions.* Then say the *Our Father* from memory, followed by the *prayer* given in the Proper of Saints. Conclude with "May the Lord bless us, etc."

**Daytime Prayer**

Begin with "God, come to my assistance, etc." The

*antiphon* and the *reading* (according to the appropriate hour) are given in the Proper of Saints, and the *psalms* are taken from the "current weekday," which is usually of Psalter Week IV.

☑ If Christmas occurs on a Saturday, then the Solemnity of the Holy Family, on Sunday, December 26, will begin Psalter Week I. Consequently, the "current weekday" of December 27 will be the Monday of Psalter Week I.

Note that only one antiphon is given in the Proper of Saints for each hour of the Daytime Prayer; in cases such as this, the antiphon serves for all three psalms. Therefore, recite the antiphon, then say each psalm, each followed by the *Glory to the Father*, and then conclude by reciting the antiphon again. Turn back to the Proper of Saints for the *prayer*. Conclude with "Let us praise the Lord, etc."

**Evening Prayer II**

☑ If December 27 occurs on a Saturday and the Holy Family occurs on the following day, a Sunday, then Evening Prayer I of the Holy Family is said.

Begin with "God, come to my assistance, etc." In the Proper of Seasons, you are told to take the *hymn, an-*

*tiphons, psalms and canticle* from Evening Prayer II of Christmas, page 414. Then return to the Proper of Seasons for the *reading and responsory*. The *antiphon* for the Canticle of Mary is given in the Proper of Seasons as well. You must turn to the Ordinary for the Canticle of Mary itself. Turn back to the Proper of Seasons for the *intercessions*. Then say the *Our Father* from memory, followed by the *prayer* given in the Proper of Seasons. Conclude with "May the Lord bless us, etc."

## Night Prayer

Take everything from Night Prayer, using the section for "Night Prayer following Evening Prayer II."

# ABOUT THE AUTHOR

Raymond Lloyd Richmond, Ph.D. holds his doctorate in clinical psychology and is licensed as a psychologist (PSY 13274) in the state of California.

Previous to his doctoral degree, he earned an M.A. in religious studies, an M.S.E. in counseling, and an M.S. in clinical psychology.

During the course of his education he received specialized training in Lacanian psychoanalysis, psychodynamic psychotherapy, cognitive-behavioral therapy, and hypnosis. He completed a Post-doctoral Fellowship in Health Psychology.

His clinical experience encompasses crisis intervention; treatment for childhood emotional, physical, and sexual abuse; trauma and PTSD evaluation and treatment; and treatment of psychotic, mood, and anxiety disorders.

33820508R00104

Made in the USA
Middletown, DE
29 July 2016